WADSWORTH-PHILOSOPHERS SERIES

ON

SOCRATES

Hope May
Central Michigan University

Wadsworth
Thomson Learning.

Australia • Canada • Mexico • Singapore • Spain
United Kingdom • United States

Printed in the United States of America
1 2 3 4 5 6 7 03 02 01 00 99

For permission to use material from this text, contact us:
Web: http://www.thomsonrights.com
Fax: 1-800-730-2215
Phone: 1-800-730-2214

For more information, contact:
Wadsworth/Thomson Learning, Inc.
10 Davis Drive
Belmont, CA 94002-3098
USA
http://www.wadsworth.com

ISBN: 0-534-57604-4

WcST END

Table of Contents

Preface

This book discusses the essentials, both historic and philosophical, regarding Socrates and his philosophy. Insofar as Socrates' philosophy is concerned, I concentrate mainly on Socrates' method, and the importance of this method (and its results) to self-knowledge, morality, and human happiness. Whereas the first chapter is more historical than philosophical, it allows the reader to understand some of the political factors that may have played a role in Socrates' trial that are too often ignored. In addition, I take up the "Socratic problem," i.e., the problem of determining who the historical Socrates was on the basis of the conflicting testimonies of Aristophanes, Plato and Xenophon. The accounts of all three authors are discussed, and reasons are given in support of regarding the testimony of Plato as the most accurate.

Socrates' trial and defense is the topic of chapter two. Socrates addresses two sets of accusations at his trial, the earlier, informal ones, and the more recent formal accusations. Both sets of accusations are discussed, as is Socrates' refutation of all of them. In chapter two we learn about Socrates' life, why he believes that others have misperceived him, and why he defends the philosophical life.

In chapter three, the mechanics of the Socratic *elenchos*, Socrates' method, are discussed. The reader learns about the three different logical techniques utilized by Socrates in his refutation of others: 1) demonstrating the consequences of a belief, 2) showing that one has inconsistent beliefs, and 3) refutation by counterexample. Examples from Plato's early dialogues show the reader how Socrates employs all of these techniques. The benefits of the Socratic *elenchos* are also mentioned in chapter three. The reader will learn that the *elenchos* helps one to eliminate false beliefs and inconsistencies in one's belief set, and that it also helps one to sharpen their moral concepts. I also comment on the benefits that these results have on one's moral perception, and this topic extends into chapter four, in connection with Plato's *Crito*. For in chapter four, the argument between Socrates and Crito about Socrates' escape, is seen to be a disagreement regarding their moral perception, rather than their moral principles. And the reader sees that Socrates' discussion with Crito, changes Crito's understanding about whether it would be right for Socrates to escape. Some of the important features of Socratic ethics are discussed and briefly contrasted with the our conception of morality.

This book can be read on its own, or as a supplement to Plato's dialogues. There are both review questions and discussion questions at the end of each chapter to facilitate classroom discussion. The book would work quite well in an introduction to philosophy course. For the features of Socrates' philosophy that I discuss: his logical method of refutation, and its effect on human understanding and perception, are features of philosophy in general.

I am indebted to many people for helping me to develop the account of Socrates that is outlined in this book. Most notably is Nicholas Smith, from whom I have learned so much. I have also benefited from my conversations with Peter Asquith, Eric and Maria Boals, Jason Ellenburg, Jordan Lindberg, Mark McPherran, Joe Martin, Philip May, Phyllis and Michael Muench, Paul Neufeld, Nadine Pullar-Karlsen, Michael Russo, Joe Salerno, and many students at both Michigan State and Central Michigan University. Finally, this book is dedicated to Daniel Kolak, for his love and devotion to philosophy and to his students, and for helping me to remember.

Introduction

Although he claimed to possess no wisdom great or small, Socrates has ironically given the Western world some of the most important insights about the human condition. It was painfully clear to Socrates that most human beings know very little about themselves. Even you, who are comfortably reading these words, believe that you know yourself better than anyone else. For unlike others, you have direct access to your thoughts, beliefs, desires and dreams, and you think therefore, that in knowing your inner states, you know yourself. It is someone exactly like you whom Socrates would have shown to be seriously mistaken. No one, claimed Socrates, can even start to know themselves unless they lead an examined and philosophical life. For it is only through self-examination by which human beings can start to see behind the thoughts, beliefs, desires and dreams, that they wrongly think are their own. For behind the cognitive states that you think are yours, there is something else, something breathing, something alive that can only be known by philosophy. This is who you are, and to know this is to know yourself. This is what Socrates tried to teach his fellow Athenians. And he was condemned to death for doing so.

If you understand Socrates' story, you understand something very sad and tragic indeed. For Socrates put his finger on the problem with human beings, and lived his entire life trying to remedy it.

1

Socrates believed that although human beings could never be fully wise, and know themselves completely, they could nevertheless know *a lot* about themselves if they just tried. And Socrates believed that if human beings could just get a glimpse of who they really are, then they could mitigate human suffering significantly. This is the message that Socrates preached on the streets of Athens, and in the space of the agora. And this is the message that, in the end, caused Socrates' fellow Athenians to condemn him to death.

Socrates gave to human kind not only invaluable moral insights, but also clear illustrations of the power of human reason and thought. Socrates used and perfected logical techniques on his and others' views about moral rightness and wrongness. And today, these same techniques are ubiquitously used not only in philosophy, but also in legal jurisprudence and the sciences.

But although Socrates' logical techniques are alive and well in the twentieth century, his moral views, and his views about human nature are not. This is unfortunate, since Socrates had important insights into the nature of morality that have largely been forgotten today. Most forgotten, are his views about the relationship among reason, perception and morality. It has taken us too long to realize what Socrates, Plato, and Aristotle realized so long ago, that our perception of the world is mediated through our own concepts and beliefs, and that our perception of the moral dimensions of the world can be mistaken due to false beliefs and inaccurate concepts.

In an age of moral relativism and post-modernism, where many human beings believe that moral truth is in the eye of the beholder, and that everyone is right and no one is wrong, Socrates' views have gone out of fashion. Socrates believed that there was a moral truth that held for all human beings, and that if one did not live by it, one acted wrongly. Socrates was no relativist. But Socrates' ideas seem silly to many people today. Some people even believe that the faith that Socrates put into human reason was pathological, and that morality has nothing to do with reason. And even if there is a truth, it is thought, it cannot be comprehended by human beings. This idea is not new, it existed even in Socrates' day. In fact Socrates, and his great student Plato, were reacting against it. They offer an alternative, an alternative that too few of us know about. The alternative is that there is a truth, that it is in you, and that to know it, one needs to examine oneself and others.

Learning about Socrates' way of looking at ourselves is thrilling and stimulating. Something about it seems so very right, as it is simple and innocent. For in order to examine and know yourself, you do not need a formal education, or special training of any sort, you only need to be able to ask yourself questions about your own moral views, and to understand what your answers to them mean. Indeed, Socrates' alternative is so simple and innocent that the Athenian youth not only understood it, but tried to teach it to their elders. And, for this reason, you will learn, Socrates was accused of corrupting the youth.

If you knew Socrates, he would ask questions only for you, and he would show you that your answers reveal something mysterious and enigmatic. For he would show that your answers are reflections of something inside of you that you that you do not know. But it is disturbing that Socrates' fellow Athenians did not want to know this *at all*. And they went to miraculous lengths in order to convince themselves that it wasn't there. For they tried Socrates for being an irreligious corrupter of youth, found him guilty, and sentenced him to death.

To learn about Socrates is to learn about two tendencies within every human being. The tendency to strive for the improvement and perfection of one's rational self, and the tendency for one to avoid, fear and hate this part of oneself. Socrates realized that such disharmony existed within most human beings, and he realized that it was painful. And he sought to save others from their own self-inflicted pain by exhorting them to live the examined life. His story is one of tenacity, love, and hope, and one that resonates with our lives even today.

In what follows you will learn about Socrates, about how others have perceived him, and about how he perceived himself. You will learn about why he so zealously pursued self-knowledge, and how he did so. Most importantly, you will learn about whether you agree with Socrates' views, or whether you disagree. In either case, the important thing to ask yourself at the end is, Why?

1

Who Was Socrates?

Socrates: A Religious Reformer and Corrupter of Youth?

Approximately 400 years before the birth of Jesus Christ, Socrates (469-399 B.C.) was sentenced to death by an Athenian jury. Indicted by three different individuals: Anytus, who represented the politicians and professional men of Athens; Meletus, who represented the poets; and Lycon, who represented the public speakers, Socrates was found guilty of failing to worship the gods of the Athens, of worshipping new gods, and of corrupting the Athenian youth. These charges were serious indeed, and Socrates was found guilty of all of them at his trial. Even though an old man at the time of his trial (Socrates was seventy), the Athenians punished Socrates with death. Socrates died, in part, by his own hand. For a common method of execution during ancient times was forcing the prisoner to drink a concoction made with a poisonous plant called "hemlock." Approximately one month after his trial, Socrates died in his prison cell after ingesting this poisonous drink.

Note that Socrates was a senior citizen at the time of his trial! The fact that Socrates was punished so severely, even at such an old age, shows that he deeply disturbed the Athenians. For Socrates would have died in a relatively short amount of time, even if he had not been sentenced to death. Nevertheless, the Athenians were obliged to sentence Socrates with the death penalty, even at such an old age.

What did Socrates do that so disturbed the Athenians? According to Meletus, one of Socrates' accusers, Socrates was the *only* man in all of Athens who intentionally corrupted the youth (*Apology* 25a). Indeed, the fact that Socrates' accusers represented several different professional groups in Athens: poets, politicians, public speakers, and craftsmen, shows that Meletus was not the only one who had this perception of Socrates. Socrates' accusers saw him as truly wicked indeed. In their eyes, Socrates was a serious threat to the well being of Athens since he had the power to make others evil.

Was Socrates a Benefit to Athens?

On the other hand, some Athenians thought that the accusations against Socrates were mistaken, and therefore that his trial and death were unjust. These citizens believed that rather than making people evil, Socrates actually helped and improved others. The most eloquent defender of this view is Plato (428-347), who was a disciple of Socrates. The historian Xenophon (428-354), who was also a contemporary of Socrates, likewise believed that Socrates helped others. According to Plato and Xenophon, Socrates helped others by cross-examining and showing weaknesses in their moral views.[1]

To be sure, it is not immediately clear how the examination and criticism of one's moral views can be helpful. And most people would be quite irritated if someone criticized their moral beliefs. Imagine conversing with someone who continually pointed out the weaknesses in your beliefs. It is not a stretch of the imagination to think that it would be both painful and frustrating to pass time with such a person. So why did Plato and Xenophon think that Socrates helped others with his cross-examinations and refutations? Later on, when we discuss Socrates' method, the *elenchos*, we will why Plato, Xenophon, Socrates (and others) believed that, despite any pain and frustration that might result from being cross-examined and refuted, such an activity could help human beings in a profound way. Presently, we simply need to point out that Western history has sided with Plato's and Xenophon's understanding of Socrates. Rather than perceiving Socrates as someone who intentionally made others evil, we understand Socrates as one who not only benefited his fellow Athenians, but who has also

5

benefited many others living thousands of years later. Socrates' positive influence touches us even today.

Socrates in the Twentieth Century

Today, some 2400 years after his trial and death, Socrates is regarded as a martyr, as a sage, and as one of the most important moral philosophers in history. Universities and libraries throughout the world have buildings inscribed with Socrates' name or with his likeness. The "Socratic method," an educational method inspired by Socrates' manner of inquiry and investigation, is used in universities and professional schools worldwide. Such reverence is a far cry from seeing Socrates as someone who intentionally turned others from good towards evil! Clearly, Socrates is revered in the modern world, more than two thousand years after being condemned to death by the Greek city that was the birthplace of democracy -- the "rule of the people." [2]

Thus, rather than perceiving Socrates as a wicked corrupter of youth, like Plato and Xenophon, we eulogize Socrates and perceive him to be an individual who was devoted to the "true political craft" -- the improvement of others. We praise Socrates for his zealous pursuit of truth, and for the faith that he placed in human reason and thought – for he believed that rational inquiry and examination could help human beings to live better, happier lives. And the Western world looks upon Socrates as one of those rare individuals who dies for the sake of their principles. For you will learn later that although Socrates had the opportunity to escape and avoid his death sentence, he decided to remain in prison and accept his punishment.[3]

Plato's and Xenophon's view of Socrates, then, rather than the view of Anytus, Meletus, and Lycon, has seriously influenced our own understanding of the man. According to both Plato and Xenophon, Socrates' accusers were wrong to bring formal charges against him.

Nevertheless, it is indeed curious that Socrates was perceived so differently by his friends and disciples, on the one hand, and by his accusers, on the other. Why did some individuals see Socrates as a threat to Athens, and why did others see him as one of Athens' greatest benefactors?

Was Socrates A Political Threat to Athens?

One explanation of why some people perceived Socrates to be a threat to Athens, concerns his political connections. For Socrates' relationships with several individuals who were political enemies of Athens might have contributed to the perception that he was a threat to this city.

Socrates' trial occurred at a time in which Athens had recently undergone significant political change, due to their loss to the city of Sparta[4] in the Peloponnesian war (431-404 B.C.).[5] Sparta was an oligarchy -- a city in which a select group of individuals ruled the citizens. Since approximately 507 B.C., however, Athens had been a democracy – a city in which the citizens made their own rules.[6] However, not all Athenians supported democracy. In fact, several Athenian aristocrats thought not only that the majority of men were simply not qualified to make political decisions, but also that the freedom that democracy affords to its citizens actually corrupts human beings. Plato, one of Socrates' disciples, writes in his *Republic* that democracy ruins the character of human beings by failing to properly train their appetites or desires.[7] That is, democratic citizens desire sex, food, and wealth more than they desire the perfection of their souls, which is what all human beings truly desire, according to Plato. Democracy corrupts human beings, because it is the government of the poor, uneducated and corrupt, and the leaders of this form of government, who are immoral rather than virtuous, spread their licentiousness to others in their polity. Plato and many other Athenian aristocrats impugned democracy for these reasons.

After their victory, the Spartans made use of the Athenian opposition to democracy and replaced Athens' democracy with an oligarchy, known as "The Thirty Tyrants."[8] These tyrants were Athenian aristocrats who were hostile to democracy,[9] and some of these men were friends with Socrates.[10]

Effective opposition against the Thirty enabled Athenian democrats to restore democracy in 403 B.C., only a year after oligarchy had been established.[11] Anytus, one of Socrates' accusers, had an important role in restoring democracy to Athens.

Thus, in 399 B.C., when Socrates was brought to trial, Athens had been a democracy for only four years. The fact that democracy had been recently reinstated at the time of Socrates' trial, could have very well been one of the reasons why Socrates was perceived to be a threat to democratic Athens. Probably, the Athenian democrats wanted to purge Athens of individuals who were threatening to the new democracy. Since Socrates was connected with some of the members of the Thirty, he could have very well been seen as such a threat.

Socrates and Alcibiades

In addition to his connection to the Thirty tyrants, Socrates' relationship to the Athenian general Alcibiades (450-404) is another factor that could have contributed to the perception that he was a threat to Athens. Alcibiades actually betrayed Athens when he sided with the Spartans in the Peloponnesian war. Although Alcibiades eventually returned to Athens, hostilities rose against him as Athens started to lose the war to Sparta. Eventually, Alcibiades was despised by both the Athenians and the Spartans. Xenophon describes Alcibiades as "exceeding all in licentiousness and insolence" (*Memorabilia* 1.2.12).

Both Plato and Xenophon indicate that Alcibiades and Socrates were sexually intimate.[12] Although Socrates was married to a woman named Xanthippe, evidence strongly suggests that he was also sexually intimate with Alcibiades. Sexual relationships between males were much more accepted in ancient Greek society than they are accepted in the United States today.[13] These relationships usually involved an older male and another male who was much younger. In this case, Socrates was the elder, and Alcibiades the younger (Alcibiades was nineteen years younger than Socrates).[14]

Given that Alcibiades was a tactless and unscrupulous traitor to democratic Athens, Socrates' relationship with him couldn't have been favorably perceived by the Athenians. Alcibiades was surely not a faithful democrat, and he had fought with the Spartans against Athens. Indeed, the relationship between Socrates and Alcibiades most likely contributed to the perception that Socrates was a threat to democratic Athens

Why Socrates' Trial was Not Completely Political

Socrates' association with several political undesirables might cause one to reasonably conclude that his trial and conviction were completely political. Were the actual charges against Socrates -- corrupting the youth, worshipping false gods, and not worshipping the gods of the state -- used to conceal the political nature of his trial? Was Socrates tried and convicted solely because of his political connections?

It is unlikely that Socrates' trial was completely political. For one

8

thing, after democracy was restored, the Athenian democrats granted amnesty to the survivors of the Thirty. So if Athenian democrats were unwilling to execute actual members of the Thirty, then it is highly unlikely that Socrates was condemned to death because of his mere connection to this group. Why would the Athenians condemn Socrates to death, on the one hand, when they allowed the remaining members of the thirty to survive, on the other? Moreover, it appears as if Socrates supported democracy rather than oligarchy. For Plato tells us that Socrates not only fought valiantly for democratic Athens during the Peloponnesian war,[15] but also that Socrates disobeyed the Thirty on at least one occasion.[16] In addition, Socrates enjoyed the free speech that was afforded by Athenian democracy, as it allowed him to publicly cross-examine and refute others.

There is not strong evidence, then, for thinking that Socrates' trial was completely political. Therefore, we have no reason to believe that the formal charges of Anytus, Meletus and Lycon, were fabrications. Indeed, political factors might have *contributed* to the perception that Socrates was a threat to Athens, but they were definitely not the whole story. The evidence points to the fact that Socrates' accusers, as well as the professional groups whom they represented, perceived Socrates to be much more than a mere political threat to Athens. Presumably, Socrates was perceived to be a threat to Athens not only because he associated with certain political undesirables, but also because he was perceived to be a religious reformer who had the power to make others evil.

The Socratic Problem

That Socrates was unfavorably perceived is certain. But why did his accusers perceive him to be a religious revolutionary and a corrupter of youth? Were Anytus, Meletus and Lycon correct in their estimation of Socrates? Or did Socrates benefit Athens? Unfortunately, it is no easy matter to answer these questions. For Socrates wrote nothing. There is no library in the entire world that possesses a single book, a single page, or even a single sentence authored by Socrates. Consequently, we are forced to know about Socrates through the testimonies of others. However, it is notoriously difficult to construct a portrait of Socrates from these testimonies since they disagree in fundamental respects about his words and deeds. There are difficulties in determining who Socrates was, and what he did that so disturbed the Athenians.

Although many people have written about Socrates, there are only three extant testimonies written by individuals who actually knew him. We have already mentioned Plato, one of Socrates' disciples. Plato wrote in a dialogue form, with Socrates appearing as a principal character in most of these dialogues. We have also mentioned Xenophon (428-354). An historian by trade, Xenophon wrote a collection of reminiscences about Socrates entitled *Memorabilia*, in addition to a dialogue entitled *Symposium* in which Socrates' views are discussed. In addition to the testimonies of Plato and Xenophon, a character named "Socrates" appears in the comic play *The Clouds*, written by the comic poet Aristophanes (450-385).[17]

However, Plato, Xenophon, and Aristophanes, give conflicting accounts of Socrates. Consequently, it is not clear *what* Socrates did. This makes it difficult to determine who Socrates was, and why he was perceived to be a religious reformer and a corrupter of youth.

Who Was the "Historical" Socrates?

Let's refer to the actual Socrates about whom we want to know as the "historical Socrates," and distinguish the historical Socrates from the "Socrates" that appears in the works of Plato, Xenophon and Aristophanes. It is impossible that Plato, Xenophon and Aristophanes all accurately portray Socrates, since their accounts contradict one another. For instance, in his comic play *Clouds*, Aristophanes portrays Socrates as a paid teacher and an atheist who is interested in scientific matters. In *Clouds*, Socrates is interested in explaining rain, thunder and other natural events, and he states explicitly that Zeus does not exist.[18] In the writings of Plato and Xenophon, however, Socrates is not a paid teacher,[19] is not interested in scientific issues, and is not an atheist.[20] Xenophon explains that Socrates eschewed the study of the heavens because he thought such studies were of little value.[21] And this is corroborated by Plato's account. In Plato's dialogue *Phaedrus*, for instance, Socrates claims that science is of no value to him, since it does not enable him to "know himself."[22] According to both Plato and Xenophon, Socrates was primarily interested in *moral* questions, rather than in scientific or naturalistic ones.[23] Plato's and Xenophon's account of Socrates, then, contradicts Aristophanes' account in significant ways.

Scholars refer to the difficulties in trying to learn about the historical Socrates from these contradictory accounts as "The Socratic Problem." The Socratic problem has existed since antiquity, and continues to be a source of scholarly controversy today.[24]

If we want to know who Socrates was, and what he did that led people to perceive him to be a religious revolutionary and a corrupter of youth, then we are faced with the task of determining which of our main authors most accurately depicts him. Whose account is more accurate? Plato's? Xenophon's? Aristophanes'? Like Akira Kurosawa's great film *Rashomon*,[25] which chronicles four conflicting testimonies of a single event (thus illustrating the difficulties that obtain in discovering the Truth), we are forced to discover the "Truth" about the historical Socrates on the basis of several conflicting testimonies.

Why Aristophanes Does Not Depict the Historical Socrates

So where do we start in determining who the historical Socrates actually was? Well, there are good reasons for believing that the "Socrates" in Aristophanes' *Clouds* is not an accurate depiction of the historical Socrates. For one thing, although there are portions of Plato's and Xenophon's account that disagree with one another, there are, nevertheless, some portions of these accounts that are in agreement.

As mentioned earlier, both Plato and Xenophon claim that Socrates was neither a paid teacher nor an atheist, and that he was concerned with morality and human welfare, rather than with scientific or naturalistic questions. And so Aristophanes is alone in claiming that Socrates was a paid nature philosopher. Moreover, both Plato and Xenophon agree that Socrates helped people by cross-examining them. Aristophanes, however, portrays Socrates as a bungling fool, useful to no one. Aristophanes' Socrates is concerned with absurd and trivial matters. For instance, in *Clouds*, Socrates is concerned with the question of how many "fleafeet" a flea can jump, as well as with the nature of the gnats' digestive system![26] Such concerns are ridiculously trivial indeed, and are a far cry from spending one's time with the improvement of others through cross-examination and refutation, which is how both Plato and Xenophon describe Socrates. The fact that Aristophanes' account has no corroboration, and the fact that some portions of Plato's and Xenophon's are mutually corroborative, is evidence that Aristophanes' depiction of Socrates is not historically accurate.

A further reason for thinking that Aristophanes does not accurately depict the historical Socrates, is that Aristophanes' Socrates appears as a character in a comic play. One should be cautious about using a work of comedy as the primary basis for an account of the historical Socrates, or of any other historical figure, for that matter. Think of the many spoofs of George Bush or Bill Clinton that you have seen on television. Surely one would be misguided if their understanding of these men were primarily based on such spoofs. To be sure, comic sketches do often have a factual basis, for if they did not, then the joke would be ineffective. But the factual basis on which a humorous caricature is based is often superficial and distorted. President Clinton may enjoy eating fast food, for instance, but this is very different than hoarding the meals of others, which is the story line of one well known Clinton caricature. Since a comic sketch of an individual is typically a distortion of that individual, then it is reasonable to assume that Aristophanes' comic portrayal of Socrates is a distortion.[27] And since it is likely that Aristophanes portrayal of Socrates in *Clouds* is a distortion, we have another good reason for believing that the testimony of Aristophanes is not a completely accurate account of the historical Socrates.

If we can eliminate the testimony of Aristophanes as an accurate description of the historical Socrates, the "Socratic problem" is narrowed down to just two authors: Plato and Xenophon. Are there any reasons, then, for thinking that either the testimony of Xenophon or Plato is a more accurate depiction of the historical Socrates? Indeed there are.

Plato or Xenophon?

Although the testimonies of Plato and Xenophon agree with one another in certain respects, there are portions of these two testimonies that are in disagreement with one another. Xenophon, for instance, claims that Socrates was devout and pious throughout his life.[28] Plato's Socrates, on the other hand, appears to endorse religious beliefs that are revolutionary and novel. The fact that Plato and Xenophon give divergent accounts of Socrates' religious behavior, is extremely important since two of the formal charges against Socrates mention his religious views. Socrates, recall, was formally charged with failing to worship the gods of Athens, and with worshipping false gods.

Xenophon on Socrates' Religious Views

Xenophon claims that Socrates did nothing irreligious. In fact, Xenophon goes to great lengths to describe Socrates as law abiding and pious. Xenophon's Socrates engages in the traditional religious rituals and sacrifices of Athens, and in Xenophon's *Memorabilia,* Xenophon claims that Socrates never did anything but *obey* the religious customs of Athens:

> First, then, for his attitude towards religion; his deeds and words were clearly in harmony with the answer given by the Priestess at Delphi to such questions as "What is my duty about sacrifice?" or about "cult of ancestors." For the answer of the Priestess is, "Follow the custom of the State: that is the way to act piously." And so Socrates acted himself and counseled others to act. To take any other course he considered presumption and folly. (*Memorabilia* 1.3.1)[29].

Thus, Xenophon portrays Socrates as utterly conventional in his religious views. According to Xenophon, all of Socrates' religious behavior conformed to the laws and customs of Athens.

Socrates' Divine Sign

Given that Xenophon's Socrates does nothing impious, how does Xenophon explain why others perceived him to be irreligious? In the *Memorabilia*, Xenophon claims that Socrates had a "divine sign," a prophetic voice that told him what to do and what not to do.[30] Xenophon claims that Socrates' divine sign is responsible for the charge that he worshipped new gods:

> First then, that he rejected the gods acknowledged by the state -- what evidence did they produce of that? He offered sacrifices constantly, and made no secret of it, now in his home, now at the altars of the state temples, and made use of divination with as little secrecy. Indeed it had become notorious that Socrates claimed to be guided by 'the divine sign.' It was out of this claim, I think, that the charge of bringing in strange deities arose. (*Memorabilia.* 1.1.2).[31]

Xenophon goes on to defend Socrates by claiming that Socrates' divine sign was no different than the sign that prophets, soothsayers, and other religious professionals experienced.[32] In claiming this, Xenophon

13

attempts to acquit Socrates of the charge that he worships novel gods. For according to Xenophon, Socrates acknowledged the same sorts of gods that were acknowledged by religious professionals in Athens. And these religious professionals were not only commonplace, but were also respected. Just as prophets gave advice on the basis of divine voices that they heard, so too, did Socrates.

Why Xenophon Believes that Socrates was Perceived to be a Religious Reformer

As you have seen, Xenophon describes Socrates as having nothing but conventional religious views. Socrates conformed to the religious orthodoxy in Athens, and was gifted with the "divine sign" that prophets and other religious professionals experienced. Why, then, was Socrates charged with irreligious behavior? Xenophon's answer is that, the Athenians misunderstood Socrates' divine voice. For the Athenians thought Socrates' divine voice was something different from the divine voice heard by prophets, oracles, and other religious professionals. According to Xenophon, however, Socrates divine voice was no different that the voices heard by the religious authorities in Athens.

Plato on Socrates' Religious Views

Like Xenophon, Plato indicates that Socrates' divine sign was responsible for the charge that he worshipped novel gods. At one point in Plato's dialogue, *Euthyphro*, Euthyphro claims that Socrates is being charged with worshipping false gods because of his divine sign. He says to Socrates, "it is because you say that you always have a divine guide that Meletus is prosecuting you for introducing religious reforms" (*Euthyphro* 3c).[33] The claim that Socrates' divine sign was responsible for the charge that he worships new gods, is an important area of agreement between Plato and Xenophon.

Plato on Socrates' Divine Sign

However, Plato portrays Socrates' divine sign rather differently than Xenophon. For Plato indicates that Socrates' divine sign only spoke to him when he was about to do something wrong. That is, according to Plato, Socrates' divine sign only tells him what *not* to do,

14

not *what* to do. In Plato's *Apology*, Socrates claims that he did not pursue a political career because his divine voice told him not to do so:

> It may seem curious that I should go around giving advice like this and busying myself in people's private affairs, and yet never venture publicly to address you as a whole and advise on matters of state. The reason for this is what you have often heard me say before on many other occasions—that I am subject to a divine or supernatural experience which Meletus thought to travesty in his indictment. It began in my early childhood—a sort of voice which comes to me, and when it comes it always dissuades me from what I am proposing to do, and never urges me on. It is this that debars me from entering public life. (*Apology* 31c-e)[34]

Plato, then, indicates that there was something different about Socrates' divine voice. For it only stopped Socrates from doing certain things, rather than giving definitive advice about what to do. But this disagrees with Xenophon's claim that Socrates' divine voice told Socrates what not to do *and* what to do. In fact, the reason why Xenophon believed that Socrates' divine sign was no different than the signs witnessed by the religious authorities of Athens, was because Socrates' sign gave definitive advice about what to do. Remember, Xenophon sees Socrates as sort of prophet, as someone who gives counsel on the basis of the divine voice that he hears. But this is the very thing that Plato denies. According to Plato, Socrates' divine sign only tells him what not to do. Consequently, Plato's Socrates is not like a prophet. For he does not give advice based on his divine sign. According to Plato, then, Socrates' divine voice was something different from the voices heard by the religious authorities of Athens.

Plato on Socrates and Religious Tradition

There is a further difference between Xenophon's and Plato's account of Socrates' religious views. For unlike Xenophon's Socrates, the Socrates in Plato's early dialogues does not engage in traditional religious rituals. In fact, in Plato's dialogue the *Euthyphro*, Socrates claims that he does not believe in the traditional stories about the gods. After Euthyphro states that he believes that the traditional story about Zeus enchaining his own Father, Socrates states:

> There Euthyphro you have the reason why the charge is brought against me. It is because, whenever people tell such

stories about the gods, I am prone to take it ill, and so it seems, that is why they will maintain that I am sinful. (*Euthyphro* 6b)

In this passage, Socrates admits that he does not believe some of the traditional stories about the gods, and he also explains that this is why others have charged him with not believing in the gods of the Athens. This is, of course, very different than Xenophon's claim that Socrates did nothing but obey the religious precepts of Athens!

Plato's Euthyphro: Socrates' Novel View About the Relationship Between the Gods and "Holiness"

A further point by which Plato indicates that Socrates had unconventional religious views, concerns Socrates' views on the nature of holiness.

In Plato's dialogue *Euthyphro*, Socrates and Euthyphro meet in front of the courthouse at Athens. Socrates is there to see the formal charges against him that Meletus has posted on the side of the courthouse. Euthyphro is there because he is prosecuting his own father for murder. For one of the slaves belonging to Euthyphro's father had killed another slave in a drunken brawl. Euthyphro's father, in order to prevent the drunken slave from doing further harm, bound and gagged him and threw him in a ditch. Meanwhile, he sent someone into town in order to figure out what should be done about the murderous slave. The slave, however, had died in the ditch whilst Euthyphro's father was waiting for word. And for this reason, Euthyphro is prosecuting his father for murder.

Socrates is incredulous after hearing this story. Indeed, it is not at all clear that Euthyphro's father *murdered* his slave, as murder is intentional, malicious killing. It seems that the slave *accidentally* died in the ditch. Socrates points out to Euthyphro that he must be certain that prosecuting his father is the right thing to do, lest he risks angering the gods. Euthyphro tells Socrates that he is quite confident that he is doing the right thing! And once Socrates hears this, he asks Euthyphro to share his knowledge about rightness and holiness. As Socrates notes, if Euthyphro knows, with certainty, that prosecuting his father for murder is holy and righteous, then he should be able to explain what holiness is, and *why* prosecuting his father is the right thing to do. So Socrates asks Euthyphro to define "piety" or "holiness." Socrates repeatedly asks Euthyphro to state the one thing – the essence –

16

common to all and only holy things.

Although Euthyphro tries several times to state what holiness is, Socrates finds problems with each of his claims. And although no substantial definition of "holiness" is reached, Socrates does say something very interesting and indeed novel about "holiness."

At one point, Euthyphro defines holiness as "what all the gods love". Socrates scrutinizes this definition and realizes that it is ambiguous – that it can mean more than one thing. For what is not clear is the nature of the relationship between holiness, on the one hand, and the gods' love of holiness, on the other. For, something could be holy just because all the gods love it. On the other hand, the gods could love something *because* it is holy. And so after Euthyphro defines holiness as "what all the gods love," Socrates asks "is what is holy, holy because the all the gods love it, or do all the gods love it because it is holy?" (*Euthyphro* 10a). In other words, is Euthyphro's indictment of his father holy because the gods love it, or do the gods love Euthyphro's indictment because this act is holy? Both Socrates and Euthyphro agree that the second alternative is the correct one – the gods love certain actions, including Euthyphro's, *because* they are holy. And this indeed is a revolutionary religious claim, as it implies that *holiness is not defined in terms of the gods*.

Since the above is a terribly important but somewhat subtle claim, let us take a moment to get clear on the point that Socrates is making. Consider the question that he asks Euthyphro: "is what is holy, holy because the gods love it, or do the gods love it because it is holy?" Not even Euthyphro fully understands this question immediately after Socrates asks it. Euthyphro's response to Socrates after hearing the question is "I do not get your meaning" (*Euthyphro* 6b). So to make Socrates' question easier to understand, let's ask the same question about something a bit more concrete than "holiness."

Think about the shape of a square for a moment. To be sure, there are things that are square shaped, and there are things that are not square shaped. *But is something square shaped because we say it is, or do we say that something is square shaped, because it is, in fact, square shaped?* If the first alternative is true, then something is square shaped *just because we say it is*. In other words, if, for instance, we say that a football is square shaped, then it is. But this seems wrong indeed. Just because we say that a football is square shaped does not mean that it *is* square shaped. For the football has the shape that it does regardless of what we say about it.

Consider, then, the second option – i.e., that we say that something is square shaped because it is, in fact, square shaped. This option acknowledges that the shape of an object does not depend on anything that we might say about that object. Moreover, if we do say that an object is square shaped, it is because we recognize the property "being square shaped" is instantiated by that object.

The question "is what is holy, holy because the gods love it, or do the gods love it because it is holy?" asks whether "holiness" is just whatever the gods say it is, or whether "holiness" is a property that the gods recognize. Again, is Euthyphro's action holy *just because* the gods love it, or do the gods love Euthyphro's action because it is holy? That is, do the god's recognize that the property "holiness" is a characteristic of Euthyphro's act of prosecuting his father?

In asking whether "holiness" is a property that the gods recognize, Socrates is asking whether "holiness" is independent of the gods *in the same way that being "square shaped" is independent of us*. The general question that Socrates asks concerns the question of why certain properties (such was being square shaped) are predicated of certain objects (such as the face of a die). Do objects have the properties that they do just because we say so, or do we ascribe certain properties to certain objects because those objects *in fact* possess those properties? Our intuitions tell us that we ascribe certain properties to certain objects because those objects possess those properties. Socrates points this out to Euthyphro. For something is not holy just because the gods say it is. Rather, *just as we say that the face of a die is square shaped because the face of a die is square shaped, the gods love holy actions because those actions are holy.*

In the *Euthyphro*, then, Socrates makes a novel religious claim. For he claims that "holiness" exists *independently* of the gods, although the gods can recognize this property. This is tantamount to saying that "goodness" exists independently of the Judeo-Christian God, although this God can *recognize* goodness. Goodness, in other words, is "out there," and is independent of God. It is as if "goodness" and God are two different pieces of "furniture in the world," *but goodness is one thing, and God is another*. Socrates and Euthyphro agree that holiness is one thing, and the gods are another. Socrates does not want to know about the *relationship* that these two things have to one another. Rather, Socrates wants to know what holines*s is*. What is *that* piece of furniture, that thing, holiness? What is it like? In Socrates' time, these questions were not commonplace. For it was thought that holiness

18

depended on the gods, and that to be holy, one simply did things that pleased the gods. But Socrates is saying that holiness is something independent of the gods, a claim that not even Euthyphro, a famous priest, can understand.

Why Plato believes that Socrates was Perceived to be a Religious Reformer

According to Plato, then, Socrates did indeed have unconventional moral views. Socrates divine voice merely told Socrates what *not* to do, and this set Socrates' divine experience apart from the divine experiences had by prophets and other holy persons. Moreover, Plato's Socrates does not believe in the traditional stories of the gods. Finally, in Plato's *Euthyphro*, Socrates indicates that he thinks that holiness exists independently of the gods -- the gods are one thing, and holiness is another.

Plato versus Xenophon Revisited

Recall our question of whether there are reasons for preferring either the account of Plato or Xenophon as an accurate depiction of the historical Socrates. We have now seen that that there are better reasons for preferring Plato's account over Xenophon's. For if Xenophon's account of Socrates is correct, then it is difficult to understand why Socrates was formally indicted with being a religious reformer. For Xenophon's Socrates does absolutely nothing that would lead one to reasonably conclude that he was a religious revolutionary, or even a threat to Athens. True, perhaps the Athenians misunderstood Socrates' divine voice, but it is not clear why they did. If, as Xenophon says, Socrates counseled others on what to do, then why did the Athenians believe that Socrates' divine voice was different than the divine voice heard by prophets and other holy persons? Xenophon provides no answer.

On the other hand, Plato's Socrates behaves in ways that explain why Athenians would have perceived him to be irreligious. Not only does Plato's Socrates disbelieve some of the traditional stories about the gods, but he also believes that holiness exists independently of the gods. Furthermore, Plato's Socrates is subject to a "divine experience," unlike the divine experiences of religious persons in Athens.

Thus, whereas Xenophon's Socrates is conservative and rather unthreatening, Plato's Socrates is revolutionary. Indeed, if one keeps

19

Plato's testimony of Socrates is mind, one can begin to understand why Socrates was charged with engaging in irreligious behavior.

Plato's account of Socrates, then, allows us to understand why Socrates was perceived to be a religious reformer. However, it is very difficult to make sense of Socrates' indictment if we assume that Xenophon's testimony is accurate. Rather than being a religious revolutionary, Xenophon's Socrates does nothing irreligious at all. Since it is difficult to understand how Xenophon's Socrates could have posed a threat to Athens, Plato's account of Socrates should be preferred.

Plato's Dialogues

Although there are good reasons for believing that Plato most accurately depicts the historical Socrates, there is a further problem. For Plato does not give a consistent portrait of Socrates. That is, Plato portrays the character named "Socrates" in several different ways throughout his dialogues. In some of Plato's dialogues, Socrates is primarily concerned with exposing the weaknesses in the moral views of his interlocutors and refrains from discussing his own moral views. In other dialogues, however, Socrates is primarily concerned with espousing his own metaphysical views, i.e., views about the nature of reality, of meaning and of truth. Given that Plato portrays Socrates in different ways throughout the dialogues, it is not clear which of Plato's portrayals most accurately depicts the historical Socrates.

This problem can be solved by assuming that in some of the dialogues, Plato uses Socrates' character as a mouthpiece for his own views. Although Plato *originally* started to write his dialogues in order to chronicle the historical Socrates, eventually Plato started to write dialogues that were devoted Plato's actual philosophical views. Presumably, writing about the historical Socrates caused Plato to formulate and write about his own views in response to the questions with which Socrates was concerned. Thus, character "Socrates" is portrayed differently in Plato's dialogues because in some of them, Plato is writing in order to chronicle the actual Socrates, whereas in others, Plato uses the character "Socrates" as a mouthpiece for his own philosophical views.

Plato's Early Dialogues

20

The dialogues in which the character "Socrates" corresponds to the historical Socrates are referred to as the "early" dialogues. This is because we believe that Plato was writing about the historical Socrates early on in his career, and that later on in his career, Plato was writing about *his own views*, rather than those of Socrates. Accordingly, we refer to the dialogues in which Plato appears to express his own philosophical views as the "middle" and "late" dialogues.

In the early period dialogues which include *The Apology, Crito,* and *Euthyphro,* among others, Socrates is a principal character. The Socrates in the early dialogues is concerned with the definitions of moral terms such as "virtue," "holiness," and "courage." Rather than defending his own views, the Socrates in Plato's early dialogues is more concerned with the views of his interlocutors.

In the early dialogues, Socrates repeatedly asks his interlocutor – the person with whom is speaking – to define some moral term by stating the "one thing common to all and only holy things," for instance. Socrates then cross-examines this definition and shows that it is problematic.

Although Socrates is a master of showing the weaknesses in the views of others, he repeatedly denies that he possesses wisdom in the early dialogues. This is curious. But as you will read in chapter three, Socrates means something very specific by "wisdom". And once you Socrates means by wisdom, you will understand why he disclaims that he is wise, even though he is so adept at showing the weaknesses in the moral views of others

Given that Socrates repeatedly exposes the weaknesses of others' moral views in the early dialogues, the early dialogues typically end with Socrates' interlocutor in a state of perplexity and even discontent. This is because Socrates' interlocutor is usually confident that he possesses knowledge and wisdom about the topic under consideration. For instance, in the Plato's dialogue *Euthyphro,* Euthyphro is convinced that he knows what holiness is until Socrates proves otherwise. And when he realizes that Socrates can expose the weaknesses in his beliefs about holiness, Euthyphro is confused and ashamed. In fact, at the end of the dialogue, Euthyphro walks away from Socrates, although Socrates wants to continue the discussion. This sort of scenario is common in the early dialogues.

Importantly, the Socrates in Plato's early dialogues behaves in ways that explain why he was formally indicted by the Athenians. We have already discussed the different ways in which Plato's Socrates has unconventional religious beliefs. But the Socrates in Plato's early dialogues also behaves in ways that explain why others perceived him to be a corrupter of youth.

Although Socrates would cross-examine and refute anyone willing to talk to him, the Socrates in Plato's early dialogues often cross examines and refutes *experts*, people who were presumed to be wise and knowledgeable about some subject. It is certain that these individuals found Socrates' cross-examinations and refutations extremely annoying, and even offensive. Imagine if someone cross-examined and refuted everyone and anyone, and most notably, experts and persons of influence. Cross-examining and refuting the Pope, Hilary Clinton, Bill Gates, and others, for instance, would surely anger these people and their supporters. And if these individuals were revealed to be ignorant about the very areas on which they were supposed to have expertise, this would certainly be damaging to their reputations. This is in fact what Socrates does in Plato's early dialogues – he shows that people who are regarded as being experts in a certain area, are in some sense ignorant about that area. Imagine if someone today showed that the Pope did not know what holiness was, and that Hilary Clinton did not know what a human right was (she is a recognized expert on the rights of children), and so on. The credibility of the Pope and of Hilary Clinton would be seriously undermined.

Socrates' refutations of others were public. Socrates would walk around in the "agora," the public meeting place at Athens, cross-examining and refuting people whom others regarded as wise. Many Athenians saw him do this, even the youth of Athens, who, according to Socrates, enjoyed watching their superiors cross-examined and refuted. In fact, the youth realized by watching Socrates, that they too could cross-examine and refute their superiors. In Plato's *Apology*, which is a report of Socrates' trial, Socrates claims that one of the reasons why others are angered at him is because from him, the youth have learned to question and refute their superiors:

> There is another reason for my being unpopular. A number of young men with wealthy fathers and plenty of leisure have deliberately attached themselves to me because they enjoy hearing other people cross-questioned. These often take me as their model, and go on to try to question other persons. Whereupon, I suppose, they find an unlimited number of people who think that they know something, but in fact really know little or nothing. Consequently, their victims become

22

annoyed, not with themselves, but with me, and they complain that there is a pestilental busybody called Socrates who fills young people's heads with wrong ideas. (*Apology* 23c-d).

The Socrates in Plato's early dialogues taught the Athenian youth how to question and refute their superiors. And when the young men in Athens realized that they could do this, and hence that their parents, professors, and priests were not wise, they most likely became irreverent and disobedient. For if the one's superiors do not know anything special, then why should they be taken seriously? Why should they be obeyed?

Thus, the account of Socrates in Plato's early dialogues enables us to see not only why Socrates was perceived to be a religious reformer, but also, why he was perceived to be a corrupter of youth. He was perceived to be a religious reformer because he followed a strange divine voice, because he did not believe in the traditional stories about the Athenian gods, and because he had a novel view of "holiness." And he was perceived to be a corrupter of youth because he taught young people how to refute their superiors.

Socrates was indeed aware that others perceived him as a threat to Athens. However, he thought that others' perception of him as a religious reformer and a corrupter of youth was *incorrect*. In fact, in refuting others, Socrates did not intend to humiliate them, but to help and improve them. Let us now turn to Socrates' defense of himself against the accusations as depicted in Plato's *Apology*, so that we can begin to see why.

Questions for Review:

1. What were the formal charges against Socrates?
2. What reasons do we have for thinking that Socrates' trial was primarily political?
3. Why is it wrong to think that Socrates' trial was completely political?
4. Who are our primary sources on Socrates?
5. What is the "Socratic Problem"?
6. Why is Aristophanes' description of Socrates in *Clouds*, disregarded as being an accurate depiction of the historical Socrates?
7. What are some similarities between Plato's and Xenophon's account of Socrates?

8. What are the main differences between Xenophon's and Plato's account of Socrates?

9. Why should Plato's account of Socrates be regarded as more accurate than Xenophon's?

10. In what way does Plato's Socrates endorse novel religious views?

Discussion Questions

1. Both Plato and Xenophon believed that Socrates helped others when he cross-examined and refuted their moral beliefs. In your view, what benefit, if any could be produced by examining and criticizing one's moral views?

2. Socrates was charged with being a corrupter of youth. What, in your view, does it mean to be a corrupter of youth? Are there any persons or influences in today's society that you believe "corrupt the youth"? If so, what are they and what, if anything, should be done about them?

3. Based on what you have read about Socrates so far, do you think that he posed a threat to the well being of Athens? Why or why not?

Endnotes

[1] Although both Plato and Xenophon describe Socrates' cross-examinations, Plato gives a much more detailed description of them than does Xenophon.

[2] The democracy of Athens was very different than the democratic system that operates in the United States. The democracy in the U.S. operates by means of elected representatives – congresspersons who represent the various districts within a state; and senators who represent a single state. The democracy in Athens was non-representative, however. Rather than electing officials to represent the people, the people (which included only Athenian born men) represented themselves.

[3] According to Plato's dialogue *Crito*, several of Socrates' close friends had prepared for his escape. According to the *Crito*, Socrates chose not to escape because the *reasons* for doing so were not strong. See chapter four in this book for discussion.

[4] Many students confuse the one city of Athens with all of Greece. There is some truth to this insofar as Athens became the dominant city

of Greece because of their successful leadership during the Persian wars. But many different cities and colonies comprised ancient Greece. Sparta and Athens were among the most powerful of Greek cities.

[5] The Peloponnesian war primarily arose because Athens' power and influence threatened Sparta. The success of Athenian commerce, and the fact that Athens had led several successful military expeditions against Persia, enabled Athens to dominate other Greek cities, economically, intellectually, and morally. Sparta was naturally suspicious of Athens' power, and so waged war with this great city for 27 years. Sparta was the victor in this long war.

[6] Not everyone who lived in Athens was a citizen – foreigners (those who were not born in Athens), women, and slaves were excluded from citizenship. Inspired by ancient Athens, the founding fathers of the United States adopted a definition of citizenship similar to that of Athens. Thus, both Athens and the United States (for some time), excluded women and slaves from political participation.

[7] See Book 8 of Plato's *Republic* 557a-562a.

[8] Xenophon in *Hellenica* 2.3.2 lists the Thirty by name: Polychares, Critias, Melobius, Hippolochus, Eucleides, Hieron, Mnesilochus, Chremon, Theramenes, Aresias, Diocles, Phaedrias, Chaereleos, Anaetius, Peison, Sophocles, Eratosthenes, Charicles, Onomacles, Theognis, Aeschines, Theogenes, Cleomedes, Erasistratus, Pheidon, Dracontides, Eumathes, Aristoteles (not the philosopher), Hippomachus, Mnesitheides.

[9] The Thirty were not just merely hostile to democracy – they employed the common tactics of ruthless leaders, killing those who were their political enemies.

[10] In particular, Critias, the leader of the Thirty, was friends with Socrates. See Xenophon's *Memorabilia* 1.2.12 and 1.2.24. Critias appears as a character in Plato's early dialogues *Charmides* and *Protagoras*, as well is in the late dialogues *Critias* and *Timaeus*.

[11] The Spartans agreed to restore democracy because they realized that it was futile to establish an oligarchy in Athens. Shortly after the Thirty had assumed power, faithful democrats led a coup that resulted in the death of several of the tyrants, including Critias.

[12] See 1.3.10 in Xenophon's *Memorabilia* and 217c-d in Plato's *Symposium*. See note fourteen for a fragment from Plato's *Symposium*.

[13] Women were degraded in Greek society, and seen as nothing more than vessels for procreation and sources of sexual pleasure. Consequently, romantic love between a man and a woman was thought to be less valuable than love between two men. For only men were considered to be fully human and rational, and therefore, it was only love between two man wherein a relationship between two rational beings could be found. For the ancients, the love between two rational beings was the highest kind of love.

[14] In Plato's dialogue *Symposium*, Alcibiades explains his frustration in trying to seduce Socrates. There is an element of irony in Alcibiades' story because it was customary in ancient Athens for the older male to desire the younger male much more than the younger desired the older (for the younger was more beautiful than the older). But according to Alcibiades (the younger), the desire that he had for Socrates was stronger than the desire that Socrates had for him. In fact, there is a double irony here. For Alcibiades was regarded as extremely handsome, whereas Socrates was not:

> ...I used to go and meet him, and then, when we were by ourselves, I quite expected to hear some of those sweet nothings that lovers whisper to their darlings when they get them alone—and I liked the idea of that. But not a bit of it! He'd go on talking just the same as usual till it was time to go home. So then I suggested we should go along to the gymnasium and take a bit of exercise together, thinking that something was bound to happen there. And would you believe it, we did our exercises together and wrestled with each other time and time again, with not a soul in sight, and still I got no further. Well, I realized that there was nothing to be gained in that direction, but having put my hand to the plow I wasn't going to look back till I was absolutely certain how I stood; so I decided to make a frontal attack. I asked him to dinner, just as if I were the lover trying to seduce his beloved, instead of the other way round. It wasn't easy, either, to get him to accept, but in the end I managed to (*Symposium* 217b-d).

Translation is by Michael Joyce.

[15] In Plato's dialogue entitled *Laches*, Laches, a distinguished Athenian general, states that Socrates fought valiantly at Laches' side in the battle at Delium (*Laches* 181b). And in Plato's *Symposium*,

26

Alcibiades, expresses similar sentiments as he discusses the time when he and Socrates were soldiers at both Potidea and Delium (*Symposium* 220a-221b).

[16] In the *Apology* 32b-d, which is a report of Socrates' defense, Socrates states that when the Thirty ordered him to fetch Leon of Salamis for execution, he disobeyed. In this passage, Socrates also claims that the Thirty were evil, and this shows that he did not sympathize with the tactics of this group.

[17] The great philosopher Aristotle (384-322), who was Plato's student for 20 years, also mentions Socrates. Aristotle, however, was born 17 years after Socrates' death. Since Aristotle did not have first hand knowledge of Socrates, scholars do not consider him to be a primary source on Socrates. Aristotle's account of Socrates is similar to Plato's account of Socrates in the early dialogues.

[18] See pp. 50-51 in *Clouds*, found in *Four Plays by Aristophanes 1994*, Meridian. Translated by William Arrowsmith.

[19] At 19e in Plato's *Apology*, Socrates claims that he is not a paid teacher. This claim is corroborated at 1.2.60 in Xenophon's *Memorabilia*.

[20] See 23b-c in Plato's *Apology*, where Socrates claims that he philosophized in Athens in order to obey the God Apollo's divine command. 1.3.1-1.3.4 in the *Memorabilia* are some of the many passages in which Xenophon implies that Socrates was not an atheist.

[21] For instance, Xenophon writes:

> [Socrates] strongly deprecated studying astronomy so far as to include the knowledge of bodies revolving different courses, and of planets and comets, and wearing oneself out with the calculation of their distance from the their periods of revolution and the causes of these. Of such researches, again he said that he could not see what purpose they served. He had indeed attended lectures on these subjects too; but these again, he said, were enough to a lifetime to the complete exclusion of many useful studies (*Memorabilia* 4.7.5).

See also *Memorabilia* 4.7.6. All translations of the *Memorabilia* are by E.C. Marchant.

[22] See *Phaedrus* 229d-230b.

[23] Aristotle also claims that Socrates was interested in moral questions, rather than scientific ones. See his *Metaphysics* 987b.

²⁴ The chief debate is between those who side with Leo Strauss' view that Xenophon depicts the historical Socrates, versus those who side with Gregory Vlastos' view that Plato's early dialogues depict the historical Socrates. Strauss' book *Xenophon's Socrates*, describes in detail Xenophon's testimony of Socrates. Thomas Brickhouse's and Nicholas Smith's *Plato's Socrates*, describes in detail Plato's testimony of Socrates in the early dialogues.

²⁵ Kurosawa's film *Rashomon* is an adaptation of the short stories "Rashomon" and "In the Woods", by Ryunosuke Akutagawa. In Kurosawa's film a woman is raped and a man murdered. However, the event is presented entirely in flashbacks from the perspectives of four narrators: the raped woman, the murdered man, the alleged murderer, and an "impartial observer." Although there are some similarities in these four descriptions, there are also important differences.

²⁶ In the following excerpt from *Clouds*, Socrates is portrayed as ruminating on the athletic abilities of the flea. A prospective student, Strepsiades, has come to join Socrates' school, called the "Thinkery." After he enters he talks to one of Socrates' pupils, who informs him about Socrates' latest discovery:

> Student: Listen. Just a minute ago, Socrates was questioning Chairephon about the number of fleafeet a flea could broadjump. You see, a flea happened to bite Chairephon on the eyebrow and then vaulted across and landed on Socrates' head.

> Strepsiades: How did he measure it?

> Student: A stroke of absolute genius. First he melted some wax. Then he caught the flea, dipped its tiny fit into the melted wax, let it cool, and lo! little Persian booties. He slipped the booties off and measured the distance.

> Student: Lord Zeus, what exquisite finesse of mind!

See pp. 32-33 in *Clouds*, found in *Four Plays by Aristophanes 1994*, Meridian. Translated by William Arrowsmith.

²⁷ Accordingly, the scholarly consensus is that in *Clouds*, Aristophanes tries to make a point about the Athenian intellectuals *in general*, and he uses a character named "Socrates" to do so. Socrates, after all, was an intellectual with whom many Athenians were familiar. And a comic sketch of an individual is much more effective if that

individual is well known.

[28] See 1.1.20 and 1.3.1-1.3.4 in the *Memorabilia*.

[30] Xenophon claims that Socrates used his "divine sign" to counsel others on what to do, and on what not to do:

> Many of his companions were counseled by him to do this or not to do that in accordance with the warnings of the deity: and those who followed his advice prospered, and those who rejected it had cause for regret. (*Memorabilia*. 1.1.4).

See also Xenophon's *Apology* 4.8.1.

[31] Translation is by E.C. Marchant.

[32] Xenophon describes Socrates as no different than a commonplace prophet of Athens, such as Euthyphro:

> He was no more bringing in anything strange than are other believers in divination, who rely on augury, oracles, coincidences and sacrifices. (*Memorabilia*. 1.1.3)

[33] All translations of *Euthyphro* are by Lane Cooper.

[34] See also 40b in the *Apology*. All translations of the *Apology* are by Hugh Treddenick.

2
The Trial of Socrates

Plato's *Apology*

Socrates was formally charged with corrupting the youth, with worshipping false gods, and with failing to worship the gods of Athens. An actual trial was held in 399 B.C in which Socrates defended himself.

Plato's *Apology* (which here means "defense" rather than "an acknowledgement that one is sorry") is an account of Socrates' trial.[1] The *Apology* is one of the few Platonic dialogues in which Socrates speaks about his own beliefs and actions. For in Plato's early dialogues, as you now know, Socrates cross-examines the moral views of others while refraining from extensively discussing his own. In the *Apology*, however, Socrates not only speaks about some of his own beliefs, but he also defends his actions -- indeed his life -- against the charges of his accusers. Thus, the *Apology* offers much more information about the historical Socrates than some of Plato's other early dialogues. The *Apology* contains Socrates' explanation and defense of the life that he led. The *Apology* is Socrates' defense of *himself*.

In chapter one we discussed some of the reasons why Socrates was perceived to be a religious reformer and a corrupter of youth.

Namely, that Socrates not only had unconventional moral views, but that he also taught the youth to cross-examine and refute their superiors. For these reasons (and perhaps for others), Socrates was perceived to be a religious reformer and a corrupter of youth. In his defense, Socrates argues that these perceptions of him are false, and hence that the formal accusations against him are groundless.

Let us now turn to Socrates' actual defense of himself, as found in Plato's *Apology*.

The Earlier, Informal Accusations

Socrates defended himself very thoroughly at his trial. Believing that the formal accusations against him had been the result of a "false impression that had been the work of many years" (*Apology* 19a), Socrates addresses this misperception and claims that there are really two sets of accusations that he needs to address. On the one hand he must defend himself against the formal accusations made by Anytus, Meletus, and Lycon. On the other hand, however, he must defend himself against the misperceptions that others long ago had of him. Socrates refers to these older accusations as "informal" charges, since these older charges were not actually legal indictments as were the charges of Anytus, Meletus, and Lycon. Rather, these older accusations were simply the unfavorable perceptions that others had of Socrates. But Socrates believes that even something as "informal" as unfavorable perceptions can be very powerful and dangerous.

Socrates mentions the informal accusations because he believes that they have given rise to the more recent, formal accusations made against him. Thus, Socrates believes that unfavorable perceptions from long ago, ultimately caused Anytus, Meletus, Lycon, and the several professional groups whom they represented, to formally indict him.

In his defense, Socrates argues that these former perceptions of him are incorrect. And he also argues that these perceptions were passed on to future generations, who subsequently were mistaken in their understanding of Socrates. One might say that in the same way, racism is passed on from generation to generation in our own time. For people who are prejudiced against certain races perceive the members of these races to be "inferior," and this perception is typically passed on to their children, to their children's children, and so on. Socrates states that, in like manner, false perceptions of him have been passed on from generation to generation, and have

31

ultimately led to the formal indictment against him. At his trial, Socrates states how he was perceived by others long ago:

> Let us go back to the beginning and consider what the charge is that has made me so unpopular, and his encouraged Meletus to draw up his indictment. Very well, what did my critics say in attacking my character? I must read out their affidavit, so to speak, as though they were my legal accusers: Socrates is guilty of criminal meddling, in that he inquires into things below the earth and in the sky, and makes the weaker argument defeat the stronger, and teaches others to follow his example. (Apology 19b-c)

These charges are shorthand for saying that others perceived Socrates to be a *naturalist* and a *sophist*. For naturalists "engaged in inquiries into things below the earth and in the sky," and sophists, as you will see, "made the weaker argument defeat the stronger." In claiming that the earlier, informal accusations against him are groundless, Socrates denies that he is either a naturalist or sophist.

Who were the Naturalists?

In charging him with "engaged in inquiries into things below the earth and in the sky," Socrates' former accusers are charging him with being a naturalist, and hence as someone who investigated questions about the universe, about the existence of the planets and stars, and about natural phenomena in general.

The naturalists were revolutionaries in their own right. For they challenged the conventional and commonplace view that natural events (such as rain, thunder, earthquakes, etc.), were the effects of the wills and intentions of the Olympian gods. Indeed, the view of the Athenian majority was that natural phenomena, such as thunder for example, was the result of Zeus' anger. The ancient naturalists, however, challenged this view. The naturalists argued that natural events should be explained in terms of natural laws or principles, rather than in terms of the intentions and wills of gods. For example, Anaxagoras (500-428), a naturalist, explained that the earth is suspended, not because it is held up by Poseidon, as some Athenians thought, but because of the resistance of the air beneath it.[2]

The Threat that the Naturalists posed to Athens

Given that the naturalists could offer explanations of natural phenomena without appealing to the Olympian gods, many perceived them as atheists, and as impious heathens. But this was typically a misunderstanding. Thales, for instance, a naturalist philosopher who explained an earthquake as "the earth rocking on water" rather than in terms of Poseidon's anger, also claimed that "everything is full of gods."[3] And, Anaxagoras, another naturalist, claimed that the world order is produced by "mind."[4] It is not clear what either Thales or Anaxagoras mean here, but it is unlikely that they are talking about the Olympian gods and goddesses such as Zeus, Poseidon and Athena. So although the naturalists were not atheists, they probably did entertain religious views that were novel and unconventional.

Nevertheless, the mistaken view that naturalists were irreligious atheists prevailed. Consequently, naturalists were impugned by many Athenians. In fact, Anaxagoras was brought to trial on a charge of impiety because of his teachings.[5] The average Athenian probably thought that the naturalists angered the gods with their secular explanations. Insofar as the Athenians perceived Socrates to be a naturalist philosopher, then they probably also believed that he was an atheist.

Who were the Sophists?

In addition to perceiving Socrates as a naturalist, Socrates' early accusers also perceived him as "making the weaker argument defeat the stronger." This accusation implied that Socrates was perceived to be a sophist.

Sophists were travelling teachers, deemed by many to be wise, who charged a fee to others in exchange for passing on their wisdom. Their services were mainly utilized by the more wealthy Athenian citizens (for only they could afford their fees) who sought political prominence. In Athens, it was necessary for one desiring political power and influence to be able to persuade others and to argue effectively in the Assembly (i.e., the main political body in Athens that functioned much like the United States Senate). Sophists were skilled rhetoricians and excellent speakers, they could effectively debate on any topic, even if they did not believe that it was true.[6] Given that the sophists were proficient in debating, it was natural for those who had political aspirations to turn to them.

Although it was reasonable enough for the Athenians to seek political training from the sophists, some criticized the belief that the sophists were adequate political mentors. Plato, surely one of the most outspoken critics of the sophists, argued that adequate political mentors should first and foremost possess knowledge of justice, and be virtuous. Plato believed that effective political leadership did not depend as much on rhetorical skill, as it depended on knowing how to tell a just decision from one that is unjust.[7]

"To Make the Weaker Argument Defeat the Stronger"

The sophists were so skilled in arguing, that they could "make the weaker claim defeat the stronger." In other words, sophists could demonstrate that out of two contradictory claims, the claim that was thought to be less plausible, had a stronger argument supporting it than the claim thought to be more plausible. For instance, consider the following two contradictory sentences:

motion is real
motion is an illusion

Most likely, the claim that "motion is real" is more plausible to you than the claim that "motion is an illusion". For your eyes tell you that motion is in fact real, and there is no apparent evidence that motion is an illusion. So, let's say that the claim that "motion is real" is the stronger claim, and "motion is an illusion" is the weaker. However, Zeno of Elea (490-430), a famous Greek philosopher who probably knew Socrates,[8] showed that the claim that "motion is real," is actually *weaker* than the claim "motion is an illusion."[9] So Zeno made the weaker claim defeat the stronger. And although Zeno was not a sophist, he was *like* a sophist, to the extent that he possessed rhetorical and argumentative skills that could make the weaker claim defeat the stronger. One famous sophist, Gorgias, who appears in Plato's important dialogue *Gorgias*, argued for the seemingly preposterous claim that "nothing is." Indeed, this claim surely seems weaker than the contradictory claim that "something is." After all, all of our experience seems to show definitively that "something is." Gorgias, however, argued that the stronger, more plausible claim is "nothing is"![10] This kind of argument was one of the sophists' hallmarks.

34

The Threat that the Sophists Posed to Athens

To be sure, the argumentative prowess of the sophists had a dizzying and stupefying (and frustrating!) effect on those who witnessed them. And although the sophists were considered to be wise, some people found them threatening and dangerous. For many sophists advocated that "there are two opposing arguments concerning everything."[11] But this claim has serious consequences. For if there are two opposing arguments concerning everything, then virtually nothing, no belief, is sacred. If the claim that "God exists" seems persuasive, for example, a sophist could argue that it is implausible. And if the claim that "God exists" did *not* seem persuasive, then the sophist could argue that it was, in fact, persuasive! It did not matter what one believed, the sophists had such sophisticated argumentative skills that they could refute anything.

Partly because the sophists believed that anything could either be argued for or against, the sophists advocated *relativism*, the idea that there is no universal, objective, human transcendent truth.[12] Even if there were a universal truth, how would we know it? Surely not through reason and argument, since any claim could, in principle, be overturned. Thus, the sophists took their ability to refute any claim as proof that there is no human transcendent truth to be known. Consequently, the sophists continually propagated the message that arguments were not tools that enabled one to discover, or get closer to the truth. Instead, the sophists put forward the view that arguments were primarily useful to one who desired to master the art of persuasion, or to one who wanted to show off and display their rhetorical skill.

The sophists' view that there is no universal, objective, human transcendent truth, was certainly disturbing to individuals who believed that there was such a truth (perhaps being found though religion, or through cultural tradition, for instance). Moreover, the sophists' brand of relativism was also certainly disturbing those who had vested interesting in having others believe that there was such a truth. The sophists, then, weren't always favorably perceived. Their revolutionary view that no claim was sacrosanct (since any claim can be refuted), posed a serious threat to the existing order and traditions of Athens. It also posed a threat for the few who believed that reason and arguments were tools by which humans could approximate or

35

even grasp the truth.[13]

Why Socrates is Neither a Naturalist nor a Sophist

According to Socrates, his earlier accusers perceived him to be a naturalist, and hence as an atheistic thinker who offered scientific explanations of natural events, rather than religious ones. Socrates' earlier accusers also perceived him to be a sophist, and hence as one who used arguments to show that any claim could be refuted, and that there is no universal, objective, human transcendent truth.

In addressing the earlier accusations against him, Socrates explains that Aristophanes' portrayal of him in *Clouds*, is partly responsible for the perception that he is both a naturalist and a sophist. For recall that Aristophanes portrays Socrates as a paid teacher and as an atheist who is concerned with scientific issues. For instance, in *Clouds*, Aristophanes portrays Socrates as having the following conversation with his pupil Strepsiades:

> Socrates: Zeus? What Zeus? Nonsense. There is no Zeus
>
> Strepsiades: No Zeus? Then who makes it rain? Answer me that.
>
> Socrates: Why, the clouds, of course. What's more, the proof is incontrovertible. For instance, have you ever yet seen rain when you didn't see a cloud? But if your hypothesis were correct, Zeus could drizzle from an empty sky while the clouds were on vacation.[14]

Thus, Aristophanes portrays paid naturalistic philosopher, and as an atheist. At his trial, Socrates explains that Aristophanes' portrayal of him is incorrect. In his defense, Socrates claims that he is not a naturalist because he in uninterested in the kinds of things with which naturalism is concerned; and he denies that he is a sophist because he has never received pay from anyone. Socrates also claims that those in the jury can testify to this fact.

> ...you have seen for yourselves in the play by Aristophanes, where Socrates goes whirling round, proclaiming that he is walking on air, and uttering a great deal of other nonsense about things of which I know nothing whatsoever. I mean no disrespect for such knowledge, if anyone is really versed in

36

it—I do not want any lawsuits brought against me by Meletus—but the fact is, gentlemen, that I take no interest in it. What is more, I call upon the greater part of you as witnesses to my statement, and I appeal to all of you who have ever listened to me talking—and there is a great many to whom this applies—to clear your neighbors mind on this point. Tell one another whether any one of you has ever heard me discuss such questions briefly or at length, and then you will realize that the other popular reports about me are equally unreliable. The fact is that there is nothing in any of these charges, and if you have heard anyone say that I try to educate people and charge a fee, there is no truth in that either (*Apology* 19c-e).

Thus, Socrates defends himself against the earlier accusations by arguing that Aristophanes' portrayal of him is incorrect – Socrates denies that he is either a naturalist or a sophist. Nevertheless, even though Aristophanes' account of Socrates is incorrect, the Athenians, after all, believed it. The crucial question is Why? This is the next question that Socrates tries to answer in his defense.

The Oracle of Delphi

Socrates explains to the jury that many people believed that Aristophanes' portrayal of him was correct because they had been angered by his cross-examinations and refutations. In his defense, Socrates explains that he cross-examined and refuted people not to anger them, but in order to understand the meaning of Apollo's oracle at Delphi. [15] Socrates' friend, Chaerephon, asked a priestess whom was believed to be a medium for the God, Apollo, Who is the wisest man in Athens? The priestess answered, "Socrates". But this puzzled Socrates. For he knew that he was not wise. Imagine if one of your professors returned from a mathematics conference, and she told you that, at this conference, you were honored for being the wisest mathematician in the entire world. Surely you would be deeply disturbed and puzzled by this, realizing that you possess little knowledge of mathematics. This is how Socrates felt upon hearing Chaerephon's story. He says to the jury:

> You know Chaerephon, of course…Well, one day he actually went to Delphi and asked this question of the god…he asked whether there was anyone wiser than myself. The priestess

replied that there was no one...Please consider my object in telling you this. I want to explain to you how the attack on my reputation first started. When I heard about the oracle's answer, I said to myself, What does the god mean? Why does he not use plain language? I am only too conscious that I have no claim to wisdom, great or small. So what can he mean by asserting that I am the wisest man in the world? He cannot be telling a lie; that would not be right for him.

After puzzling about it for some time, I set myself at last with considerable reluctance to check the truth of it in the following way. I went to interview a man with a high reputation for wisdom, because I felt that here, if anywhere, I should succeed in disproving the oracle, and pointing out to my divine authority, You said that I was the wisest of men, but here is a man who is wiser than I am.

Well, I gave a thorough examination of this person...and in conversation with him I formed the impression that although in many people's opinion, and especially in his own, he appeared to be wise, in fact he was not. Then when I began to try to show him that he only thought he was wise and was not actually so, my efforts were resented by both him and by many other people present. However, I reflected as I walked away, Well, I am certainly wiser than this man. It is only too likely that neither of us has any knowledge to boast of, but he thinks he knows something which he does not know, whereas I am quite conscious of my ignorance. At any rate, it seems that I am wiser than him to this small extent, that I do not think that I know what I do not know. (*Apology* 21 b-d).

Socrates goes on to say that after interviewing this politician, he continued to interview not only other politicians, but also others who were typically deemed to be wise, namely, the poets and the craftsmen. In each case, Socrates found the same thing: all of these individuals thought themselves to be wise, even though they were not. Socrates, however, realized that he was wiser than all of these men. For Socrates realized that he knew nothing, whereas these individuals thought they knew something, but did not.

The Meaning of the Oracle

Socrates explains to the jury that after trying to understand the oracle, and hence after discovering that those who were believed to be wise, were, in fact, ignorant, he began to understand what the oracle meant in saying that he was the wisest man in Athens:

> The truth of the matter, gentlemen, is pretty certainly this, that real wisdom is the property of God, and this oracle is his way of telling us that human wisdom has little or no value. It seems to me that he is not referring literally to Socrates, but has merely taken my name as an example, as if he would say to us, The wisest of you men is he who has realized, like Socrates, that in respect of wisdom he is really worthless. (Apology 23a-b)

Socrates realized that many Athenians mistakenly thought that they possessed wisdom, and hence failed to realize what the oracle was saying, namely, that real wisdom was the property of God alone. So Socrates concluded that the oracle singled him out as an example that illustrates that humans cannot possess wisdom.

Hostility and Anger against Socrates

It is easy to understand why Socrates' attempt to understand the oracle angered people. Time after time, Socrates would show his interlocutor that he was not wise, but ignorant. And as Socrates' examinations were public, this shamed and humiliated his interlocutors. Imagine if you were well respected by friends and colleagues for your expert knowledge of history, and imagine if you believed that you really possessed such knowledge. Surely you would be ashamed and humiliated if you were revealed to be ignorant, especially in front others who thought you were wise. Socrates recognized that his examinations may have humiliated others, but he believed that they were better off if they realized their ignorance. Nevertheless, people were very angered by Socrates.

Contributing even more to the Athenian's anger, was the effect that Socrates had on the youth of Athens. In chapter one, we mentioned that the Athenian youth liked to watch Socrates examining others, and that, by watching Socrates in the agora, the youth had learned to cross-examine and refute their superiors. Indeed, young Athenian men realized that asking the kinds of questions that Socrates asked, enabled them to expose the ignorance of their superiors. According to Socrates, the ability of the Athenian youth to question

39

and refute their superiors, intensified the anger and hostility towards him (*Apology* 23c). For everyone knew from where the youth was learning their techniques.

Many Athenians were infuriated because they were refuted not only by Socrates, but also by the Athenian youth. And it is this anger, according to Socrates, that is really behind the older, informal accusations against him. It is this anger, and this insecurity that comes with the knowledge that one is not wise, but ignorant, that compelled many Athenians to perceive Socrates as a naturalist and a sophist -- two types of intellectuals who advocated unpopular and threatening views, as we have seen. It was the Athenians' own dissatisfaction with *themselves* that caused them to believe that Aristophanes' portrayal of Socrates was accurate. Rather than facing the difficult truth that they were ignorant, and rather than taking responsibility and trying to mitigate their ignorance, the Athenians took the easy way out and claimed that Socrates was a naturalist and a sophist.

The misperceptions of Socrates as both a sophist and naturalist that were caused by Aristophanes' portrayal of him in *Clouds*, coupled with the anger and humiliation that were (inadvertently) caused by Socrates' desire to understand the meaning of the oracle, proved to be a dangerous combination. For the formal accusations against Socrates – that he corrupted the youth, worshipped false gods, and did not worship the gods of the state – were made on behalf of the professionals whom Socrates had previously demonstrated to be ignorant in his attempt to understand the oracle. Socrates' later accusers: Anytus, Meletus and Lycon, each represented a professional group that had been examined by Socrates in his attempt to discover the meaning of the oracle: Anytus represented the aggrieved craftsmen and politicians, Meletus represented the angered poets, and Lycon represented the humiliated orators. There was, in effect, a "class action" lawsuit against Socrates, chiefly incited by the anger that others felt towards him. Let us turn, then, to Socrates' defense against the more recent charges of Anytus, Meletus, and Lycon.

The Recent, Formal Accusations

Interestingly, in defending himself against the three formal charges: corrupting the youth, worshipping false gods, and not worshipping the gods of the state, Socrates refutes only two of these accusations. For Socrates does not refute the charge that he does not worship the gods of Athens. In failing to explicitly refute this charge, perhaps Socrates is acknowledging that he is guilty of it. This would make sense, given that, as we have seen, Socrates' divine voice was an unconventional religious experience. Moreover, we saw earlier that in the *Euthyphro*, Socrates not only disbelieves the traditional stories of the gods, but that he also advocates an unprecedented religious view, namely that holiness is something that exists independently of the gods. Apparently, Socrates did have unconventional religious views, and worshipped a god (or gods) that were not recognized by Athens. However, Socrates believes that the other two charges against him are false, and refutes them accordingly.

"Socrates is Guilty of Corrupting the Youth"

The first charge that Socrates addresses is that he is guilty of corrupting the youth. Socrates argues that either he does not corrupt the youth, or if he does, he does so unintentionally. In either case, Socrates concludes that a trial is not only unnecessary, but unjust.

In defending himself against this charge, Socrates cross-examines Meletus, one of his accusers. After Meletus claims that Socrates is the only man in Athens who intentionally corrupts the youth. Socrates then gets Meletus to admit that he believes that no one would want to be harmed by another. Socrates then asks Meletus:

> Am I so hopelessly ignorant as not even to realize that by spoiling the character of one of my companions I shall run the risk of getting some harm from him? Because nothing else would make me commit this grave offense intentionally. No, I do not believe it, Meletus, and I do not suppose that anyone else does. Either I have not a bad influence, or it is unintentional, so that in either case your accusation is false. And if I unintentionally have a bad influence, the correct procedure in cases of such involuntary misdemeanors is not to summon the culprit before this court, but to take him aside privately for instruction and reproof, because obviously, if my eyes are opened, I shall stop doing what I do not intend to do. But you deliberately avoided my company in the past and refused to enlighten me, and now you bring me before this court, which is the place appointed for those who need punishment, not for those who need enlightenment. (*Apology* 25e-26a).

41

In refuting the charge that he is corrupter of youth, Socrates shows that Meletus himself does not even believe that Socrates should be tried and convicted! Given that Meletus believes that no one would want to be harmed by another, then Socrates is no exception. So either Socrates does not corrupt the youth, or he does so unintentionally. Why? Because the youth would corrupt Socrates in turn, and no one, according to Meletus, would want such a thing. So, as Socrates points out, *if* he corrupted the youth, then it was unintentional. And if Socrates corrupted the youth by accident (for this is what is meant by "unintentional"), then he should be rebuked in private, not put on trial with death as the penalty. Indeed, if Socrates corrupted the youth unintentionally, then he was simply unaware of the consequences of his actions, and such ignorance surely does not warrant death as a penalty. If it did, this would be like saying that those unintentionally harm others by driving automobiles should be put to death (since automobile exhaust contains deadly carcinogens). But this is clearly absurd.

"Socrates is Guilty of Not Worshipping the Gods of Athens"

After Socrates defends himself against the charge that he corrupts the youth, he addresses the charge that he does not worship the gods of Athens. To refute this charge, Socrates asks Meletus to clarify it for him since Socrates is unsure of its meaning. Meletus states that the charge is that Socrates is a complete atheist, i.e., that he does not believe in any gods. Socrates points out that if this is what the charge means, then Meletus' indictment actually contradicts itself! For Socrates was charged with worshipping false gods *and* with not worshipping the gods of the state. But if the charge that Socrates does not worship the gods of the state amounts to the claim that he is an atheist, then surely it would be contradictory to say that Socrates is an atheist, on the one hand, and that he worships false gods, on the other. For an atheist does not worship any gods! Thus, Socrates refutes the charge that he does not worship the gods of the state (i.e., is an atheist, according to Meletus), by showing that it contradicts the charge that he worships "false" gods, which, of course, are gods of some sort.

Socrates' refutation of this charge makes use of his common tactic of getting his interlocutor to assent to a number of claims, which Socrates would then show to be inconsistent with one another. For

42

Socrates shows that given that Meletus claims that 1) Socrates is an atheist and that 2) Socrates worships false gods, he contradicts himself. When one contradicts oneself, it is reasonable to conclude that such a person is not sure of *what* they believe, and that they have not thought through their beliefs. In showing that the formal accusations against him are inconsistent, Socrates shows that Meletus has not thought through the formal accusations that he has brought against Socrates.

God's Gift to Athens

After Socrates refutes the more recent accusations of Anytus, Meletus, and Lycon, he explains to the jury that they would be wrong to sentence him to death. For Socrates believes that he is the god Apollo's gift to Athens. Socrates states that if the Athenians decide to put him to death, they will be harming the "God's gift". And this of course, would be wrong:

> I assure you that if I am what I claim to be, and you put me to death, you will harm yourselves more than me...For this reason, gentlemen, so far from pleading on my own behalf, as might be supposed, I am really pleading on yours, to save you from misusing the gift of God by condemning me. If you put me to death, you will not easily find anyone to take my place. It is literally true, if it sounds rather comical, that God has specially appointed me to this city, as though it were a large thoroughbred horse which because of its great size is inclined to be lazy and needs the stimulation of some stinging fly. It seems to me that God has attached me to this city to perform the office of such a fly, and all day long I never cease to settle here, there and everywhere, rousing, persuading, reproving every one of you. You will not easily find another one like me, and if you take my advice you will spare my life. (*Apology* 30c-31a)

Not only does Socrates tell the jury that they will suffer if they condemn the God's gift to death, but he also claims that, if he is acquitted, he will continue to examine others and to philosophize, even if he is ordered by the state not to do so:

> Well, supposing, as I said, that you should offer to acquit me on these terms, I should reply, Gentlemen, I am your very

43

grateful and devoted servant, but I owe a greater obedience to God than to you, and so long as I draw breath and have my faculties, I shall never stop practicing philosophy and exhorting you and elucidating the truth for everyone that I meet. I shall go on saying, in my usual way, My very good friend, you are an Athenian and belong to a city which is the greatest and most famous in the world for its wisdom and strength. Are you not ashamed that you give your attention to acquiring as much money as possible, and similarly with reputation and honor, and give no attention to thought to truth and understanding and the perfection of your soul?

And if any of you disputes this and professes to care about these things, I shall not at once let him go or leave him. No, I shall question him and examine him and test him; and if it appears that in spite of his profession he has made no real progress towards goodness, I shall reprove him for neglecting what is of supreme importance, and giving his attention to trivialities. I shall do this to everyone I meet, young or old, foreigner or fellow citizen, but especially to you, my fellow citizens, inasmuch as you are closer to me in kinship. This, I do assure you, is what my God commands, and it is my belief that no greater good has ever befallen you in this city than my service to my God. For I spend all my time trying to persuade you, young and old, to make your first and chief concern not for your bodies nor for your possessions, but for the highest welfare for your souls. (*Apology* 29d-30b)

Note that Socrates is claiming that human beings should really be concerned with truth and understanding, and the perfection of their souls. This is extremely important when we remember that Socrates claims that the meaning of Apollo's oracle is that humans *cannot* possess wisdom. Remember, Socrates does not believe that even *he* possesses wisdom, as he believes that real wisdom is the property of God (*Apology* 23a). But despite the fact that Socrates thinks that human beings cannot possess wisdom, he not only claims that one should concern oneself with the perfection of one's soul, but also that life is not worth living if one does not philosophize:

If I say that [not philosophizing] would be disobedience to God, and that is why I cannot "mind my own business," you will not believe me that I am serious. If on the other hand I

44

tell you that to let no day pass without discussing goodness and all the other subjects about which you hear me talking and examining both myself and others is really the best thing that a man can do, and that life without this sort of examination is not worth living, you will be even less inclined to believe me. (*Apology* 38a)

Even though humans can never attain wisdom, Socrates does not believe that the quest for wisdom is pointless. Rather, Socrates concludes from the fact that humans cannot possess real wisdom, that humans should nevertheless *try* to possess wisdom by leading the "examined" or "philosophical" life. Why did Socrates think that humans should try to possess wisdom by leading the examined life? This is a question that will be answered in the next chapter where we will discuss Socrates' method. For now, we need only to point out that although Socrates believes that humans cannot possess wisdom, they should nevertheless try to attain it.

The Examined Life

Note what Socrates implies when he says that the best thing that a human being can do is to live a life in which she examines goodness. For he agrees that wisdom is unobtainable for human beings, but he also believes that human beings would benefit in trying to obtain moral wisdom. Socrates, then, believes that it is beneficial to try to obtain a goal that is, in reality, unobtainable. Although this idea may seem silly to you, if you think about it, it is not so far-fetched as it may seem. Think about baseball for a moment. Any Major League Baseball team has to play 162 games in a season. Now it would be highly unlikely, indeed virtually impossible, for a given team to win all 162 games. But even though the goal of winning 162 games in a season is a virtually unobtainable goal, it would be foolish for the team to conclude that it is simply pointless to try to obtain that goal. In fact, it would be beneficial for the team to try to win all 162 games, for this might enable them to win the World Series!

Socrates is saying something similar about wisdom. Yes, wisdom is an unobtainable goal, but that does not mean that pursuing such a goal is pointless. In fact, pursuing the unobtainable goal of wisdom, claims Socrates, is the most beneficial thing that a human being could be doing. Socrates believes that the god Apollo has commanded him to make other human beings realize that they should

45

be trying to obtain the unobtainable goal of wisdom, and that they would benefit most of all by leading the examined life, rather than by pursuing money, fame, and political power.

This may indeed sound a little strange to you. It definitely sounded strange to Socrates' fellow Athenians, who were really quite similar to they way we behave, even two thousand years later. Like many of us, the Athenians never even dreamed that the best activity that they could undertake is trying to obtain moral wisdom. Like us, the Athenians believed that they should try to obtain money, prestige, or power instead. Realizing that his fellow Athenians were mistaken about their goals and concerns, Socrates thought that the oracle had singled him out by name, as a way of commanding him to philosophize, and to teach others the importance of leading the examined life.

Socrates believed that he was God's gift to Athens. In his mind, he was sent by Apollo to cure the Athenians – to make them realize that they should be completely focused on moral goodness, and on nothing else. Apparently, although Socrates professed ignorance, he was confident in his belief that it would be wrong for him to stop philosophizing, even if ordered by Athens to do so. And Socrates was also confident in his belief that human beings should spend their time focusing on goodness, and trying to obtain moral wisdom. Thus, Socrates tells the jury that they should honor him and thank him, rather than condemn him, as he helped the Athenians to realize that their pursuits and goals were misguided.

The Jury's Verdict

Imagine if you were one of the jurors at Socrates' trial. Would his claim that he is "God's gift" to Athens strike you with incredulity? Would you think that Socrates is being pompous and pretentious? Or would you be persuaded by what Socrates is saying? Would it seem preposterous to you that Socrates denies that he is wise, on the one hand, but claims that philosophizing is the best thing for human beings, on the other?

Well, it is no surprise as to how Socrates' jury reacted. After hearing Socrates' defense, they declared him to be guilty. There were approximately 500 jurors at Socrates' trial, all Athenian born males, and 280 had declared him to be guilty. This means that as many as 220 Athenians thought he was innocent. Socrates points out that if a mere thirty votes had gone the other way, he would have been acquitted (*Apology* 36a).

Even though Socrates was declared guilty by the majority of jurors, he had the opportunity to suggest a punishment other than death. Socrates could have proposed that his punishment should be a fine, or even exile, rather than death. For Socrates' trial was one in which the defendant had the opportunity to propose a counter penalty if found guilty. So what counterpenalty do you think Socrates proposed? He proposed that he should be rewarded! For Socrates saw himself as God's gift, and as the best thing that has ever happened to Athens:

> ...I set myself to do to you individually in private what I told you to be the greatest possible service. I tried to persuade each of one you not to think more of practical advantage than of well-being in the case of the state or of anything else. What do I deserve for behaving in this way? Some reward, gentlemen, if I am bound to suggest what I really deserve, and what is the reward which would be appropriate for myself. Well, what is appropriate for a poor man who is a public benefactor and who requires leisure for giving you moral encouragement? Nothing could be more appropriate than free maintenance at the state's expense. (*Apology* 36b).

Socrates proposes that he should not be put to death, but should be given free meals and lodging by the state. Surely some of the jurors found this to be a bombastic remark! But Socrates was not trying to provoke the jury. He was merely speaking truthfully. For he was really convinced not only that he did no wrong, but also that he was a gift from Apollo. After stating that he should be given free meals, Socrates admits that he would have proposed a fine if he had the money to do so. Socrates actually offers all that he can afford, one mina of silver. After doing so, several of his friends who are present at the trial volunteer to give Socrates some of their money, so that the fine is a more significant amount, thirty mina of silver. But the jury decided to choose the penalty of death, rather than Socrates' offer of thirty mina of silver.

Socrates states that the Athenians have sentenced him to death in order to avoid the truth that he and the Athenian youth forced them to see, namely, that human beings are ignorant and that real wisdom is the property of God alone. Socrates warns those who have voted for his death that he has created an army of other Athenians, an army of youths that he had been restraining, who will attack even more vigorously the conceit and pretense of their elders. Socrates claims that no matter what they do, the Athenians can never escape these attacks, *unless they become good.*

> You have brought about my death in the belief that through it, you will be delivered from submitting your conduct to criticism, but I say that the result will be just the opposite. You will have more critics, whom up till now I have restrained without your knowing it, and being younger they will be harsher to you and will cause you more annoyance. If you expect to stop denunciation of your wrong way of life by putting people to death, there is something amiss with your reasoning. This way of escape is neither possible nor creditable. The best and easiest way is not to stop the mouths of others, but to make yourselves as good men as you can. This is my last message to you who voted for my condemnation. (*Apology* 39c-e)

Socrates had prepared the youth of Athens to continue his work, to interrogate their parents, their professors, and their priests to show them what they did not want to face, namely that they were ignorant and that only God was wise.

After Socrates realizes his fate, he warns those who have voted for his death that they will be punished for killing the God's gift. He then tells those who voted for his acquittal not to be disconcerted about the decision. For death is a mystery to human beings, and is either one of two things, according to Socrates. Death is either nothingness or a migration of the soul from this world to another. In either case, claims Socrates, there is nothing to be afraid of. For if death is nothingess, then it is similar to nights wherein one sleeps without dreaming, and Socrates notes that such nights are welcomed. On the other hand, if death is a migration of the soul from this world to another, then Socrates reasons that this will allow him the opportunity to talk with many great individuals who have died, such as Homer, Hesiod and Achilles. And Socrates says that if death allows him to talk to Homer and Hesiod, he would be willing to die over and over, in order to do so. (*Apology* 40d-41c)

Although Socrates tried to defend himself, and explain to the jury that his concern was not to make others evil, but to help them to realize that their concerns were misguided, he was condemned to death. Apparently, the majority of jurors was unconvinced that

48

Socrates had good intentions. In their view, Socrates was an irritating and troublesome old man, who did nothing but criticize others. And in their view, Socrates was a dangerous figure, who could seduce and corrupt the youth with his public refutations of esteemed individuals. But Socrates insists that he tried to help others, and as you know, Plato and Xenophon agreed with this. In order to see why others saw Socrates as a benefactor to Athens, we need to understand what, exactly, Socrates was doing when cross-examined his fellow Athenians. Let us then turn to the topic of Socrates' method of cross-examination and refutation, the *elenchos*.

Questions for Review:

1. What were the earlier, informal accusations against Socrates?
2. Who were the naturalists and the sophists and why were they perceived to be a threat to Athens?
3. How does Socrates defend himself against the charges that he is a sophist and a naturalist?
4. Why, according to Socrates, did some Athenians perceive him to be a sophist and a naturalist?
5. What is the story of the Delphic oracle, and how does it pertain to the earlier accusations against Socrates?
6. According to Socrates, what was the meaning of the oracle's claim that he was the wisest man in Athens?
7. How does Socrates defend himself against the charge that he does not worship the gods of the state?
8. How does Socrates defend himself against the charge that he corrupts the youth?
9. According to Socrates, what did the God, Apollo, command him to do?
10. According to Socrates what is the most important thing with which human beings should concern themselves?

Discussion Questions

1. At his trial, Socrates claims that "the unexamined life is not worth living." What do suppose this claim means? Are there any reasons for thinking that it is true? Explain.
2. What do you think Socrates means when he claims that "no human being possesses wisdom, either great or small" (*Apology* 21b)? Do you agree with this claim? Why or why not?

3. The historian Xenophon claims that Socrates did not take his defense seriously, and tried to anger the court with his testimony, rather than try to save his life. What evidence is there in support of Xenophon's interpretation? Do you agree with him? Why or why not?

Endnotes

---

[1] Since Plato indicates that he was actually present at Socrates' trial, there is good reason to believe that much of the *Apology* is accurate depiction of it. As Socrates is trying to persuade the jury that he is not a corrupter of youth, he mentions several men who are present at the trial. Plato is one of the men mentioned by Socrates. See *Apology* 34a.

[2] See Hippolytus' Refutations of All Heresies 1.8.3.

[3] According to Aristotle, Thales claimed that "everything is full of gods." See Aristotle's *De Anima* (or *On the Soul*) 411a7-8.

[4] See Aristotle's *Metaphysics* 985a18

[5] Anaxagoras was acquitted, due to the influence of one of his close friends, Pericles.

[6] One famous sophist, Protagoras, went so far as to say that there is no truth or falsity, only "better or worse." According to Protagoras, it is incorrect to say the one perceives the world truly or falsely. Rather, one perceives the world in better or worse ways. See Plato's *Theatetus* 166c.

[7] Plato's *Republic* provides a detailed discussion about the traits that political leaders should possess. See especially books 3-7.

[8] In Plato's dialogue *Parmenides*, a story is recounted in which Socrates and Zeno discuss some of Zeno's arguments.

9 Zeno argued that motion from one point to another is impossible, since there are infinite number of points between any two points (say Chicago and New York). Now everyone agrees, it is impossible to cover an infinite number of points. For infinite means "having no end." But if it is impossible to cover an infinite number of points, and if there are an infinite number of points between Chicago and New York, then it is impossible to get from Chicago to New York or vice versa. Motion is an illusion. It does not exist! This was one of Zeno's many arguments which showed that the apparently "stronger"

beliefs supported by sense perception, are actually "weaker" than the seemingly implausible beliefs arrived at through reason and argument. See Simplicus' *Commentary on Aristotle's Physics* 1289, 5.

[10] See Sextus Empiricus *Against the Mathematicians* 7.65-86.

[11] Diogenes Laertius, in *Lives of the Philosophers* claims that Protagoras claimed this. (9.5.1).

[12] The sophists also advanced relativism because they realized that human beings had different perceptions of things. See Plato's *Theatetus* 152b.

[13] This was the view of Socrates, and of Plato and Aristotle, both of whom were profoundly influenced by Socrates. Today, Socrates' view that reason and argument are tools by which humans can approximate the truth, is expressed by the belief that science, because of the rational methods that it employs, marches towards the truth. The view that science employs rational methods which cause it to march towards the Truth was argued for by Karl Popper, and seriously challenged by Thomas Kuhn in his book *The Structure of Scientific Revolutions*.

[14] See pp. 50-51 in *Clouds*, found in *Four Plays by Aristophanes, 1994*, Meridian. Translated by William Arrowsmith.

[15] Oracular shrines were located throughout Athens, a priestess or *Pythia* believed to be a medium through which the god spoke would answer the questions asked by both common citizens and professional politicians. Decisions made in virtually any area of Athenian life were made after consulting the oracle.

3

Socratic Method

The Socratic *Elenchos*

You have now learned that misperceptions due to the pain, anger, and humiliation caused by Socrates' examinations of his fellow Athenians, were ultimately responsible for his trial and death. The Athenians could not and did not want to face what both Socrates and even the Athenian youth could demonstrate to them all too well, namely that despite the confidence that they had in their own views, they were, in fact, *ignorant*.

Socrates had a failsafe method of exposing the ignorance and conceit of others, and he called this method the *elenchos* (pronounced eh-lenk-us). "*Elenchos*" is the Greek word for "examination" or "test." The verb "*elenchein*" (pronounced "eh-lenk-ain"), from which the word *elenchos* is derived, not only means *to examine*, but it can also mean *to shame* or *to refute*. Socrates could do all of these things to others, and he did it with *questions*, questions that were crafted for the particular individual whom Socrates was examining. If you lived in Athens during Socrates' time, Socrates would have designed his questions just for you, and he would have showed you that your very answers to these questions, revealed that you were ignorant.

Importantly, Socrates did not ask questions that seemed difficult.

In fact, Socrates asked questions that others were completely confident in answering. Whether it was Meno's view about virtue, or whether it was Euthyphro's view about "holiness", the Athenians were always confident that they could answer the questions that Socrates posed. Before examining Euthyphro on the topic of "holiness," for instance, Socrates asks Euthyphro whether he thinks that he possesses knowledge of it. Euthyphro responds:

> Why, Socrates, if I did not have an accurate knowledge of all that, I should be good for nothing, and Euthyphro would be no different than the general run of men. (*Euthyphro* 4e)

This shows that prior to being examined by Socrates, Euthyphro is completely confident that he knows what holiness is. In Euthyphro's mind, Socrates question seems almost silly. Euthyphro thinks that *of course* he knows what holiness is. But after discussing the matter with Socrates, Euthyphro realizes that something is wrong. For despite the fact that he thinks he knows about holiness, Euthyphro cannot provide adequate answers to the questions asked by Socrates. Of course this confuses and perplexes Euthyphro, so Euthyphro states:

> Now, Socrates, I simply don't how to tell you what I think. Somehow, everything that we put forward keeps moving about us in a circle, and nothing will stay where we put it. (*Euthyphro* 11b)

And when Socrates' friend, Meno, a professor of virtue, realizes that he cannot even say what virtue is, he says to Socrates:

> Socrates, even before I met you they told me in plain truth that you are a perplexed man yourself and reduce others to perplexity. At this moment I fell that you are exercising magic and witchcraft upon me and positively laying me under your spell until I am just a mass of helplessness. If I may be flippant, I think that not only in outward appearance but in other respects as well you are exactly like the sting-ray that one meets in the sea. Whenever anyone comes into contact with it, it numbs him, and that is the sort of thing that you seem to be doing to me right now. My mind and lips are literally numb, and I have nothing to reply to you. Yet I have spoken about virtue hundreds of time, held forth often on the subject in front of large audiences, and very well too, or so I thought. Now I cannot even say what it is. In my opinion you are well advised not to leave Athens and live abroad. If you

behaved like this as a foreigner in another country, you would most likely be arrested as a wizard. (*Meno* 80a-b)[1]

Note that Meno claims that Socrates is like a sting-ray, and that he is exercising magic and witchcraft in refuting Meno's answers. Meno thinks, therefore, that it is *Socrates* that is doing something to Meno's answers. Euthyphro acts the same way. For after Euthyphro's answers are refuted, he too, goes on to say that, somehow, Socrates is playing with his statements, and that it is *Socrates* who is making Euthyphro's answers move about. But Socrates denies this, and he reminds both Meno and Euthyphro that *they themselves* both see the problems with their answers (*Meno* 80d, *Euthyphro* 11c). Socrates is doing nothing – it is Meno and Euthyphro who are stating answers that they recognize to be problematic. And insofar as Meno, for instance, understands and accepts the criticisms that Socrates is raising, Socrates is trying to show Meno that there is some part of him, that recognizes that Meno's answers are problematic. Indeed, something in Meno answered Socrates' questions, but this could not have been the part of Meno that understands why his answers are incorrect. For if it were, Meno wouldn't have given those problematic answers in the first place! It is almost as if there are two selves in Meno, one who recognizes the problems with his statements, and the other who puts forth the problematic statements. This is the point that Socrates makes to both Meno and Euthyphro. But neither of them get it. Both believe that Socrates is being a magician with their answers.

Both Meno and Euthyphro fail to see that Socrates is doing nothing but *thinking for them*. In showing that Meno's answers are flawed, for instance, Socrates is simply saying, *See Meno, if you thought about it, you would realize that there is a problem here, you would realize that this is not what you really believe, and hence that you do not really know what you believe.* But Meno does not get it, and instead thinks that Socrates is being like a sophist, and is twisting his words around, just for fun. But in thinking this, Meno avoids responsibility and is deceiving himself that he is fine, and that Socrates is some sort of sophistic wizard, who is exercising magic on Meno's words. *But it is not Socrates who is the wizard, but Meno himself.* Magically, Meno is convinced that he knows the topic under consideration, *even though part of him recognizes and understands that he does not.*

So when those like Meno and Euthyphro answered Socrates'

seemingly simple questions, Socrates would point out that, if they really looked at their answers *and thought about them*, they would realize that they did not *really* believe their answers. It is as if Socrates was showing to Meno and Euthyphro (and others) that they are hidden from themselves and do not even know it, and that the part of Meno that was offering answers to Socrates' questions was some foreign presence, *who was not even Meno,* for instance. On one occasion Socrates tells his friend Callicles, that once he properly knows himself, he will realize that he, Callicles, actually disagrees with the answers that he is providing to Socrates' questions! (*Gorgias* 495e).

So Socrates showed to others that their own answers revealed something indeed strange about them. On the one hand, they would provide an answer that they thought was fine, on the other hand, they could see with thought and reflection that it was not. Note that Socrates did not just go around saying "human beings are ignorant," hoping that his fellow Athenians would realize the truth of this statement. Rather, Socrates showed that *the Athenians' own answers* to his questions provided clear examples that illustrated that they were ignorant!

As mentioned earlier, however, Socrates most notably refuted *experts* -- individuals who not only believed themselves to be wise, but who were also deemed to be wise by others. These individuals more than any others, were thoroughly deceived that they knew things of great importance. For they had been seduced into believing the remarks and praises of others. Indeed, showing that not even experts possess wisdom, illustrated all too well that humans are not wise. For if experts are not wise, then who is? The Delphic priestess said that Socrates was the wisest man in Athens, but only because he realized that, in respect to wisdom, humans are worthless (*Apology* 23b).

Socrates' ability to refute others made some Athenians question Socrates' sincerity when he disclaimed wisdom. How can Socrates point out that the answers of known experts are flawed, if he himself lacks wisdom? At his trial, Socrates affirms that although it may seem to others that is wise, he really does not:

> ...whenever I succeed in disproving another person's claim to wisdom in a given subject, the bystanders assume that I know everything about the subject myself. But the truth of the matter, gentlemen, is pretty certainly this, that real wisdom is the property of God. (*Apology* 23a)

Socrates denies that he is wise even though he is able to show that others cannot adequately answer the questions that he asks. But why?

The key to understanding why Socrates disclaims wisdom on the one hand, even though he is able to refute the most learned expert, on the other, consists in understanding what Socrates means by the terms "wisdom" and "ignorance." As you will see, Socrates not only means something very specific by these terms, but he also uses the *elenchos* to reveal two very different forms of ignorance.

Ignorance

So far we have seen that Socrates shows that others are ignorant by demonstrating that there are problems with their answers to the questions asked by him. But it is important to keep in mind that Socrates did not ask others to answer questions about *anything* and *everything*. As you saw in chapter one, Socrates is only concerned with *moral issues*. Socrates, then, asks others to answer questions about their own views on morality, and he shows them that their own answers reveal that they are not only ignorant about morality itself, but are also ignorant about *their very own views* on the subject!

Moral Ignorance

But you should be puzzled that Socrates showed that others were ignorant because their views about morality were problematic. For how can Socrates demonstrate to human beings that their moral beliefs are problematic, and even false? How can one show that a moral belief is flawed? It is one thing to show that my belief that "Abraham Lincoln was the fifteenth president" is wrong – all I have to do is look in an encyclopedia in order to determine that this is indeed a false belief, (since Lincoln was the sixteenth president). But how can we show that someone's *moral* claim such as "capital punishment is morally wrong" is problematic? We cannot look at an encyclopedia, or at any other reference book, since people disagree about whether this claim is true or false. But suppose that we want to show that this claim is, in fact, flawed. How do we proceed? How did Socrates proceed?

Well, even though we cannot defer to a reference book in order to determine whether a moral claim is flawed, there are some philosophical techniques that we can use in order to do so. In fact, the philosophical techniques that are used by philosophers even today, are techniques that were perfected by Socrates.

Socrates uses a method of examination that makes use of very sophisticated and powerful logical techniques, in order to show that an *individual's moral* beliefs are problematic. And although philosophers still use these techniques today, they do not necessarily use them to examine an individual's moral beliefs, per se. Rather, contemporary philosophers use the logical techniques perfected by Socrates to examine theories, or points of view on a variety of issues ranging from the nature of morality to the nature of knowledge, and the existence of God. This is one of the main reasons why Socrates remains one of the most important philosophers in history. He showed to us how to examine, to analyze, and how to dissect ideas. Socrates showed us that, if properly developed, human reason can be a powerful instrument that can be used to examine beliefs and abstract ideas. The contribution that Socrates made not only to moral philosophy, but to philosophy in general, is unprecedented.

So in order to show that some moral claim is flawed, Socrates used the *elenchos* – his method of examination that makes use of logical techniques. What sorts of logical techniques does Socrates use to show that a moral claim is problematic? There are three: 1) he points out the *logical consequences* of moral claims, 2) he shows that human beings have *inconsistent moral beliefs*, and 3) he points out *counterexamples* to definitions of moral terms. Let us look more closely at what is involved in each of these different techniques.

Moral Beliefs and Their Consequences

What do we mean when we say that Socrates points out the logical consequences of moral beliefs? Well, every statement possesses a number of logical consequences, i.e., a number of other statements that must be true if that statement is true. For instance, if the statement "all men are mortal" is true, the statement "no men are not mortal" must be true. Thus, the statement "no men are not mortal" is a *logical consequence* of the statement "all men are mortal."

It is also the case that two or more statements taken together have logical consequences. Consider the two claims:

1. All men are mortal
2. Socrates is a man

.

57

If these two claims are true, then it must also be true that Socrates is mortal. The claim "Socrates is mortal" is a logical consequence of claims one and two. Both *individual claims* and *groups of claims* have logical consequences.

In order to grasp the notion of a logical consequence, it is useful to think of every statement, and every combination of statements, as having within them, hidden, implicit information -- information that can only be revealed by using *logical tools*, and by using structured and directed *thinking*. We say that the hidden, implicit information inside of each sentence, and inside of each combination of sentences, comprises their logical consequences.

Think of the familiar magic trick wherein a magician pulls a brightly colored scarf out of top hat, only to find that there are an innumerable number of other brightly colored scarves attached to it. The magician keeps pulling and pulling, only to find that there is no end to the chain of scarves. Beliefs and statements are like that. Attached to two beliefs "a" and "b," is another belief "c," and attached to belief "c," is another belief "d," and so on. But only by using logic and thought can one see the many consequences that are "attached" to a one's beliefs.

Thus, all of your beliefs have logical consequences. That is, all of your beliefs contain within them, implicit information that you have not yet realized, but that you *could* realize with the power of logic. Socrates would say that if you do not know the consequences of your beliefs, then you do not know yourself. Indeed, when Socrates points out the logical consequences of his interlocutors' beliefs, he is helping them to *know themselves*, and to realize what they really believe. Socrates is a master of using logic to show others the consequences of their beliefs. Let's look at an example.

The Consequences of Euthyphro's Beliefs

We saw in chapter one, that in Plato's dialogue, *Euthyphro*, Euthyphro prosecutes his own father for the murder of a slave. Remember, one of the slaves belonging to Euthyphro's father had killed another slave, and had died in a ditch after being bound by Euthyphro's father.

In order to convince Socrates that he is doing the right thing, Euthyphro notes that even Zeus and Cronus, two beloved Olympian gods, had enchained their own fathers for wrongs that they had committed. So Euthyphro reasons that if it is permissible for Olympian gods to enchain their fathers, then it is likewise permissible for Euthyphro to indict his father. Socrates claims that he does not believe these stories about the gods, but Euthyphro insists that they are true. The important thing to keep in mind is that insofar as Euthyphro believes the traditional stories about the Olympian gods, he therefore believes that the gods fight with one another, deceive one another and, in general, are enemies to one another.

As Socrates and Euthyphro continue to discuss Euthyphro's decision to prosecute his father, Euthyphro claims that, for an action to be holy, it has to be loved by the gods.

Socrates reminds Euthyphro that he believes that the traditional stories of the gods are true, and hence that the gods are enemies to one another. Socrates then asks Euthyphro what it is that the gods fight about, and Euthyphro claims that they fight about *moral issues*— about which actions are just, which actions are holy, and so on. Socrates notes, then, that Euthyphro believes the following two claims:

1. There is hatred and wrath among the gods.

2. The gods disagree about which actions are just and unjust, holy and unholy, and so on.

And from these two claims, Socrates is able to pull out the subsequent belief:

3. The gods disagree about which actions are holy and unholy

Socrates can pull out the above belief because it is *a logical consequence* of statements number one and two. For statement number one is saying that there is, in fact, hatred among the gods. And statement number two is saying that, whenever there is such hatred, the gods fight about serious moral issues. It follows that the gods disagree about which actions are holy and unholy, as this is a moral issue. Statement number three is a consequence of statements number one and number two. Thus, Socrates reveals to Euthyphro that he, Euthyphro, believes that the gods disagree about which actions are holy and unholy. *Socrates is doing the thinking for Euthyphro, so that Euthyphro can see what he believes.*

But Socrates does not stop here. For just as statements one and two have logical consequences, both statement three, in conjunction with Euthyphro's belief that prosecuting his father is holy, have logical consequences.

After Socrates shows that statement three is a consequence of Euthyphro's other beliefs, he then demonstrates to Euthyphro the consequences of statement three, and Euthyphro's belief that:

4. Prosecuting my father is holy

If Euthyphro believes both statement three and statement four, then he must also believe that there are some gods who actually think that what Euthyphro is doing is *unholy*. For if the gods fight about which actions are holy and unholy, and if Euthyphro believes that prosecuting his father is holy, then the gods disagree about this. *Given Euthyphro's own beliefs, he must believe that some gods think that prosecuting his father is actually unholy!* So from statements three and four, Socrates pulls out the following statement;

5. The gods disagree about whether Euthyphro's act of prosecuting his father for murder, is, in fact, holy.

Note that Socrates gets statement number five from Euthyphro's *other* beliefs by using reason and logic. Socrates has shown that if Euthyphro really believes what he has said, then in the end, he must believe that some gods do not think that prosecuting his father is holy!

Here is a summary of how Socrates shows that the claim "The gods disagree about whether Euthyphro's act of prosecuting his father for murder, is, in fact, holy" is actually contained within Euthyphro's other beliefs.

1. There is hatred and wrath among the gods.

+

2. If there is hatred and wrath among the gods, then the gods disagree about which actions are just and unjust, holy and unholy, and so on.

↓

3. The gods disagree about which actions are holy and unholy

+

60

4. Prosecuting my father is holy

↓

5. The gods disagree about whether Euthyphro's act of prosecuting his father for murder, is, in fact, holy

One of the logical skills that Socrates masters is the ability to see the logical consequences of others' beliefs. Socrates points out the consequences of the Athenians' beliefs, so that they can see what is inside of them. And more often than not, Socrates' interlocutors do not like what they see. For sometimes, Socrates shows they have *inconsistent moral beliefs*, and therefore that some of their moral beliefs must be *false*. And as you will see, after Socrates demonstrates the consequences of some of Euthyphro's beliefs, he then shows that Euthyphro has inconsistent beliefs.

Inconsistent Moral Beliefs

What does it mean to have inconsistent beliefs? Two statements are inconsistent, or contradictory, if they cannot both be true at the same time. For instance, here are three pairs of inconsistent statements:

Lying is always wrong
Sometimes, it is morally right to lie.

Socrates is virtuous
Socrates is evil

Capital punishment is an unjust form of punishment
Capital punishment is a just form of punishment

In each of these cases, it is impossible for both sentences to be true. And if it is impossible for both sentences to be true, then we can conclude that, in each of the above pairs of sentences, at least one, or possibly both of the sentences is/are false.

One of the ways in which Socrates shows that others have problematic moral beliefs, is to show that they have *inconsistent* moral beliefs. For in showing other Athenians that they have inconsistent moral beliefs, Socrates demonstrates that at least some of their beliefs must be false.

Socrates shows that Euthyphro has inconsistent beliefs. For at

61

the beginning of the dialogue, Euthyphro states that there is no doubt in his mind that prosecuting his father is holy. In other words, Euthyphro thinks that all of the gods believe that what he is doing his holy. So Euthyphro believes:

> 6. All of the gods agree that prosecuting Euthyphro's father for murder is holy

But this claim contradicts statement five, which Euthyphro must *also* believe, since it is a consequence of his other beliefs. Thus, Socrates shows that Euthyphro must believe the following two claims:

> 5. The gods disagree about whether Euthyphro's act of prosecuting his father for murder, is, in fact, holy

> 6. All of the gods agree that prosecuting Euthyphro's father for murder is holy

But these statements are clearly inconsistent with one another. Indeed, one cannot coherently say that the gods disagree about whether Euthyphro's action of prosecuting his father is holy, on the one hand, *and* that all the gods agree that Euthyphro's action is holy, on the other. For this would be an impossible state of affairs. Thus, one of the claims, or both, must be *false*. For that is the only way to avoid the contradiction. This is the point that Socrates makes to Euthyphro. So Socrates shows to Euthyphro that *he has at least one false belief.*

Note how Socrates is using the *elenchos* show that Euthyphro's moral beliefs are problematic. As we said earlier, many beliefs such as "Abraham Lincoln was the fifteenth president", can be shown to be false by demonstrating that such a belief does not jibe with the facts: all we have to do is look at an encyclopedia that shows that such a belief is false. But Socrates is not showing that Euthyphro's moral beliefs are false in *this* way. Indeed, the way in which Socrates demonstrates that Euthyphro has false moral beliefs, is very different than determining that a belief is false because it does not jibe with the facts. It is not as if Socrates is picking on *one* particular belief, and showing to Euthyphro that this single belief is false because it does not correspond to anything in reality. No, he is pointing out something about a *number* of Euthyphro's moral beliefs, and showing that they cannot all be true at the same time.

Importantly, Socrates does not tell Euthyphro *which* of his moral beliefs is false – his point is more subtle than that. Socrates merely wants him to realize that he is infected with this strange condition, that some of his very own beliefs are inconsistent with others. Socrates believes that, in the end, it is up to Euthyphro to resolve the inconsistency. And accordingly, Euthyphro decides that statement five is false. He is convinced that *all* of the gods believe that what he is doing is indeed holy. And when Euthyphro says this, Socrates asks Euthyphro the important question that we discussed in chapter one, namely, Is an action holy because all of the gods love it, or do all the gods love an action because it is holy? As you know, both Socrates and Euthyphro agree that all the gods love actions because they are holy. And this shows that, *despite what he says, Euthyphro really believes that the nature of holiness is independent of the gods' love for it!*

So one of the ways in which Socrates shows that ones moral beliefs are flawed, is by showing that one actually has *inconsistent* moral beliefs. In order to do this, Socrates elicits a number of different claims from his interlocutor, unpacks them (i.e., pulls out their logical consequences), and then shows that they are inconsistent with one another. Let's call the kind of ignorance that results from having inconsistent beliefs *inconsistency ignorance.* Although Socrates demonstrates that human beings possess inconsistency ignorance, this is not the only form of ignorance that he reveals.

Problematic Definitions

Often, Socrates shows to others that they are ignorant because they cannot provide adequate definitions of moral terms. Let's call this form of ignorance "definitional ignorance." Definitional ignorance is a form of ignorance that is different than inconsistency ignorance, as you will see. Socrates is a master of revealing both forms of ignorance.

Definitions are very important for Socrates. The one question that Socrates repeatedly asks, takes the following forms:

What is F-ness?

What is the one thing common to all and only F things?

where "F" is just a variable that stands for some moral property, whether it is holiness, virtue, or justice.

Socrates asked this question because he realized something curious about *general terms*. General terms, unlike proper names, can refer to many different things. Contrast the word "book" for instance, with name "William Jefferson Clinton." Whereas the word "book" refers to many different things, the name "William Jefferson Clinton" refers to just one. Thus, general terms refer to many different things, whereas proper names refer to only one. But Socrates realized that, when we use general terms, we are able to recognize that these terms refer to many different particular things, and hence that many different things are *instances* of that term. Consider the term "book" for instance. We recognize that there are many things to which this term refers. Some are:

1. The Bible
2. Gulliver's Travels
3. The Republic
4. Alice in Wonderland

and so on. Moreover, books come in various forms: some are hardcovered, some are soft-covered, some are books on cd-rom, others are books on tape, and so on. So there are many different *types* or *kinds* of books. But all of these types of books have something in common, *for they are all books*.

Socrates realized that, when we recognize that something is a book, we are recognizing that the object has some features that make it a book. So what is it that we are recognizing? What does everything in the above list have in common? And what do hardcovered books, soft-covered books, cd-rom books, and audio books all have in common? What features must an object have to make it a book?

Socrates was concerned with these questions as they pertained to *general moral terms*. Socrates recognized that just as all books must have something in common, so too must all just acts, for instance. Here are some instances of the general moral term, "just":

1. Obeying the law
2. Abiding by the terms of a contract
3. Treating people equally under the law
4. Arranging the inequalities in society so that they are to everyone's advantage
5. Assigning punishments that are proportional to the crimes committed.

and so on. Now Socrates reasoned that all of these acts, and any

64

others that we call "just", must have *something* in common, else, they would not all be called "just." Socrates wanted to know what *this* was. He was most concerned with the asking What do all just acts have in common?, What do all holy acts have in common?, What do all virtuous persons have in common?, and so on. In the *Euthyphro* Socrates asks Euthyphro, What is holiness? and, What is the one thing common to all and only holy actions? And in the *Meno*, Socrates asks Meno, What is virtue and what is the one thing common to all and only virtuous actions?

Socrates loved to ask his interlocutors to provide definitions of general moral terms. And when they did, Socrates could show that any definition proposed by his interlocutor was flawed. Sometimes, Socrates shows that a definition is flawed because it has consequences that are inconsistent with one's other beliefs. This is what Socrates does to some of Euthyphro's definitions of "holiness". Most of the time, however, Socrates shows that a definition is flawed because it is either too broad, to narrow or both. In other words, Socrates shows that definitions are flawed because they are subject to *counterexamples*. Think of a counterexample as an example that shows that some claim is false. So a counterexample to the claim that "all cars are red," is simply one car that is non-red. Let's see how Socrates refutes a moral definition by showing that it is subject to counterexamples.

Refutation by Counterexample

To see how Socrates proceeds in refuting his interlocutors' definitions, let's look at the *Laches*. Socrates asks Laches, What is that common quality, which is the same in all cases of courageous acts, which is called courage? (*Laches* 191e) Socrates wants to know what all and only courageous acts have in common. Laches, being a famous warrior, thinks he knows quite well what courage is, and his answer to Socrates' question is, When one remains at their post, and fights against their enemy.

Socrates points out, however, that Laches' definition is too narrow. For there are other instances of courage which do *not* involve "remaining at one's post." Laches' definition only pertains to the courage possessed by soldiers. But Socrates recognizes that there are instances of courageous acts that are performed *off* of the battlefield. As Socrates states, there are people who are courageous at sea, in disease, in poverty, in politics, and so on (*Laches* 191d). In pointing out that there are instances of courageous acts that Laches' definition fails to capture, Socrates states a *counterexample* to Laches' definition. For it excludes many other instances of courage. Laches *agrees* with Socrates that his definition is subject to counterexamples, is too narrow, and is therefore faulty.

So what does Laches do after Socrates points out to him that his definition is faulty? Laches simply changes his definition. Focusing on his idea of courage, and realizing now that he needs to provide a definition of courage that is immune to counterexamples, Laches changes his definition to "endurance of the soul." So Laches thinks that the one thing common to all and only courageous actions is "endurance of the soul." And once again, Socrates refutes Laches' definition by pointing out that it is subject to counterexamples. But this time Socrates uses a counterexample that shows that Laches' second definition is *too broad*, for not every kind of endurance is courage. As Socrates acknowledges, there can be "foolish endurance," which is evil and harmful. Courage, on the other hand, is never evil or harmful. Once again, Laches' definition is refuted. And once again, Laches agrees with Socrates that his second definition is faulty.

Note what Socrates is doing here. He asks Laches to focus on his own idea of courage, to fixate on it. Socrates then asks Laches to state the essence of the idea of courage upon which he is fixated – the one thing common to all and only courageous actions. But every time that Laches tries to put into words the idea of courage upon which he is fixated, Socrates shows that Laches cannot adequately do so! Laches is thinking about this thing, courage, but he cannot unproblematically say what it is. For Socrates shows that Laches' definitions are faulty by showing that they are too broad or too narrow *relative to Laches' own conception of courage*. Note that Socrates is not showing that Laches' beliefs are inconsistent. Rather, he is showing to Laches that Laches cannot adequately express his own idea of courage. And Laches *sees* this. For each time he understands why Socrates refutes his definition. It is as if Laches thinks that he fastens upon the right answer, but then Socrates provides a counterexample that makes Laches realizes that he is mistaken. In refuting all of Laches' definitions of "courage," Socrates demonstrates that he has definitional ignorance.

66

Self Refuting

To get a better sense of what is going on here, let's apply this usage of the *elenchos* to ourselves. Let's show that like Laches, we too possess definitional ignorance. That is, let's show that we are unable to provide an adequate definition of a term whose meaning we think we know. Let's work with a simple term, one with which we are very familiar such as "book." Indeed, it is safe to say that we know what this word means. For we know a book when we see one, and we can recognize when something is not a book. Socrates would say that when we recognize which objects are books – then we are recognizing a quality that is possessed by all and only books.

Now imagine Socrates asking you, What is the one thing common to all and only books? What is that quality that makes something a book? Do you feel confident that you can answer this question? If you do, you know how Socrates' interlocutors felt at the beginning of their conversations with him.

Think about what a book is, and about the essence of a book. With the idea in your mind's eye, now try to state the one thing, the one feature, common to all and only books.

Perhaps the first thing that comes to mind is "pages." And so we say to Socrates, The quality that makes something a book is having pages. But hopefully you can see that there are problems with this answer. For magazines have pages, and they are not books. Newspapers have pages and they are not books. Socrates would point out that our definition is *too broad*, it encompasses too much – for it encompasses non-books. Even worse, the definition is *too narrow*, for there are books on tape as well as cd-rom books, not to mention books that are only published on the internet. Yet none of these sorts of books has pages! So our first definition is both too broad and too narrow. Socrates would then ask us to try to define the term again, and so we would change our definition to something else, a definition that, hopefully, is better. Perhaps we should modify our definition to "having an author." Although this is a better definition because it includes audio, cd-rom, and internet books, since they all have authors, *it is still too broad* since short stories have authors. And every one agrees that short stories are not books. Socrates would point this out to us, and we would try again. What would we say next? Perhaps that the one thing common to all and only books is having an author and a binding. Can you find any problems with this definition? Is it too broad, too narrow, or both? Can you think of any counterexamples that shows that this definition is false? I can!

To sum up all of our attempts to say what the one thing is common to all and only books:

1. The one thing common to all and only books is having pages
   problem: too broad and too narrow
2. The one thing common to all and only books is having an author
   problem: too broad
3. The one thing common to all and only books is having an author and a binding.
   problem?

Hopefully this example gives you a better idea of how Socrates frequently refutes definitions of moral terms. Each time a definition is proposed, Socrates shows that it is either too broad, too narrow, or both, and hence is subject to counterexamples. This is how Socrates revealed that human beings had definitional ignorance. Again, one has definitional ignorance not because one has inconsistent beliefs, but because one cannot adequately put into words, one's moral concepts. In refuting our definition of what a book is, then, Socrates is not showing that we have inconsistent beliefs. Instead, he is showing that we cannot provide a definition of the term that is completely accurate.

It is indeed strange that we cannot provide an adequate definition of a book, for it seems like we know what one is. After all, you can automatically, instantaneously, and effortlessly recognize books from non-books. The idea of a what a book is, is so immediate, so tangible, yet, *we cannot say what it is.* This is the frustration and perplexity that Socrates' interlocutors felt. On the one hand it seemed very clear to them that they knew the topic under consideration, but on the other hand, they could not provide an adequate definition of it.

In showing that you cannot provide an adequate definition of "book," a term whose meaning that we thing we know, Socrates is pointing out some very strange things about you. Very strange. For although you can recognize a book from a non-book, you do not even know how you do this. Moreover, Socrates is showing you that you are providing answers that a part of you realizes are false. What is the part that is recognizing that your definitions are faulty? And why didn't *this* part provide your definitions of what a book is? These are the questions that Socrates wanted others to see and feel. And as you know, Socrates desire for others to see and feel these questions disturbed others so much, that they condemned him to death! Keep in mind that we have been using the *elenchos* on the very dull topic of what makes a book, a book. Books are easy to recognize (even though we do not even know how we recognize a book from non-book!). Furthermore, people do not disagree about which things are books, and which things are not books. But remember, Socrates was not concerned with the question, What makes a book, a book? Rather, Socrates was concerned with the questions, What makes a just act, just? and What makes a virtuous person, virtuous? And now that you have seen how difficult it is to define something as uninteresting as what a book is, imagine how much more difficult it is to try to define something much more complex such as "justice" or "virtue." For people disagree about which actions and persons are and are not just. And people disagree about which actions and persons are and are not virtuous. Not to mention that the terms "justice" and "virtue" denote something much more abstract than the word "book" does. Indeed, it is much easier to think about what makes a book, a book, than it is to think about what makes a just act, just, or what makes a virtuous person, virtuous. If we cannot say without difficulty what a book is, then we can start to understand why Socrates' interlocutors could not provide unproblematic definitions of moral terms such as "justice" and "holiness".

So far we have discussed the two different ways in which Socrates revealed the ignorance of others. On the one hand, Socrates would point out the consequences of others' moral beliefs, and would show that they were inconsistent with some of their other beliefs. When Socrates uses the *elenchos* in this way, he uses it to reveal that human beings possess inconsistency ignorance. On the other hand, Socrates would point out that others' definitions of moral terms were faulty by showing that they are either too broad, too narrow, or both. And when Socrates uses the *elenchos* in this way, he uses it to reveal that human beings possess definitional ignorance. Thus, Socrates demonstrated that there are two forms of ignorance that afflict human beings.

In claiming that he too, was ignorant, Socrates did not mean that he possessed no true moral beliefs. Rather, he meant that he could not provide adequate definitions of moral terms, and hence was definitionally ignorant. Socrates probably also meant that some of his beliefs had consequences that were inconsistent with his other beliefs.

Remember, however, that Socrates lived the examined life, and hence spent much of his life examining the moral views of himself and others. So even though Socrates was ignorant, his definitions of moral terms were not as problematic as the definitions of others, and he probably possessed fewer inconsistent beliefs than most of his fellow Athenians. Nonetheless, Socrates claimed that he was, for all intents and purposes, ignorant. And Socrates claimed that *all* human beings are ignorant in this sense, for only the God possesses wisdom.

Thus Apollo, who was among other things, the God of health, revealed to Socrates that human beings are infected with the disease of ignorance. And Socrates used the *elenchos* to demonstrate this to his fellow Athenians. Sometimes Socrates used the *elenchos* to reveal that human beings have inconsistent moral beliefs, and sometimes he used the *elenchos* to point out that human beings cannot adequately define moral terms, and hence are definitionally ignorant. Presumably, only God is wise, because only God possesses adequate definitions of moral terms, and has moral beliefs that are immune from inconsistencies.

The Benefits of the *Elenchos*

Although Socrates was able to demonstrate that human beings are afflicted by both inconsistency and definitional ignorance, Socrates also used the *elenchos* to benefit both himself and others. And when we realize what these benefits are, we will understand why Plato and Xenophon believed that Socrates benefited rather than harmed his fellow Athenians. We will understand why Socrates claimed that "the unexamined life is not worth living."

The *elenchos* was not only an instrument that enabled Socrates to reveal the malady of ignorance that his interlocutors possessed, but it was also a *therapeutic* instrument that enabled him to mitigate this ignorance. It was as if the Delphic oracle had informed Socrates of a serious illness that affected human beings, ignorance, and Socrates realized that, although the illness, could not be completely cured, it could nevertheless be put into remission with the help of the *elenchos*.

Insofar as Socrates used the *elenchos* to show others that they have inconsistency ignorance, Socrates allows others to zoom in on a segment of their belief set that is inconsistent. As you saw, Socrates does this to Euthyphro, when he points out that Euthyphro believes

70

the following two inconsistent claims:

5. The gods disagree about whether Euthyphro's act of prosecuting his father for murder, is, in fact, holy

6. All of the gods agree that prosecuting Euthyphro's father for murder is holy

Once Euthyphro sees this, he does indeed recognize that some of his beliefs must be false. And Euthyphro decides that it is statement number 5 that is false, and hence eliminates it from his belief set. In throwing out this belief, Euthyphro reduces the degree to which his moral beliefs are inconsistent, and he eliminates a belief that he believes to be false. And of course, it is indeed beneficial to reject beliefs that one realizes are false.

When Socrates demonstrated that others had definitional ignorance, there was yet another benefit that this conferred. To see this, recall our attempt to define what a book is. There were three definitions that we proposed in the following order:

1. The one thing common to all and only books is having pages
2. The one thing common to all and only books is having an author
3. The one thing common to all and only books is having an author, and a binding.

Note that each time we attempt to define what a book is, our definition is an improvement over our prior attempts. For our definitions become more and more precise with each definition attempt. The process of definition attempt, counterexample, and re-attempt causes us to think more and more about the characteristics possessed by all and only books. And as we think more and more about these characteristics, we are getting clearer and clearer on our conception of what a book is.

Although it is true that we may still fail to adequately provide a definition of what a book is, even after many definition attempts, this does not prevent us from sharpening our definition of what a book is. And insofar as repeatedly attempting to define what a book is causes us to sharpen our conception of it, the degree to which we are definitionally ignorant is lessened, mitigated.

Socrates used the *elenchos* on definitions of moral terms because it had this therapeutic affect. By forcing his interlocutor to repeatedly provide definitions of "justice," for instance, Socrates was forcing his interlocutor to sharpen this idea of this term.

The fact that the *elenchos* – that cross-examination and refutation – is beneficial in these two different ways, shows why both Plato and Xenophon believed that Socrates helped others in revealing the weaknesses in their moral views. For elenctic examination enables one to eliminate inconsistencies and falsehoods from one's belief set, to sharpen one's conceptions of moral terms, and therefore to lessen the degree to which one is ignorant.

Visual Aid

But it is quite important to point out that both eliminating the false beliefs in one's belief set, as well as sharpening one's definitions and conceptions of moral terms, also helps one to better *perceive the moral dimensions of the world.* This is a terribly important point, but one that is often over looked due to the misunderstanding that we have about the nature of perception. Most people understand perception to be a passive activity, and therefore believe that, in perceiving, one is simply aware of "what is out there." When we see the moon's reflection on water, in other words, most of us believe that our eyes are simply taking in that slice of reality. Most of us believe that we perceive reality directly, and that perceiving the world is like watching a movie -- a manifold of events happen in the world, and our senses take it all in.

In point of fact, however, perception is not a completely passive activity. The concepts and knowledge that you possess, your beliefs, expectations and your past experiences, all play a role, an important role, in determining what you perceive. Consider watching a professional gymnast in a competition with judges present. Not being a gymnast yourself, every move executed by this gymnast seems to you to be a miracle. She is remarkable. In your mind, she deserves a "10." Yet, the judges give her a 5. You are shocked, of course. But only because you fail to realize *that the judges are seeing something different than you are.*

The fact that the judges perceive something different than you do, shows that perception cannot be a completely passive activity. For if this were correct, then we would all perceive the same things. Yet, sometimes, we *disagree* about what we perceive.

The deep question is, *why* is it that we perceive things differently? Why is it that the gymnastic judges perceive a routine to be a "5," whereas you perceive it to be a "10"? *Because the judges possess knowledge and experience of gymnastics, whereas you do not.* Being trained gymnasts themselves, they know how difficult (or easy) a move may be. Each of the judges has a trained eye. Their knowledge and past experiences, enables them to see more than you -- who has no experience in gymnastics -- can see. *The knowledge and understanding that you possess determines what you see.*

But not only that. For the *general terms* that you possess determines what you see. Suppose that you are walking through a garden and you do not possess the general term "chrysanthemum". Then, when you walk past a patch of red which is, in fact, a chrysanthemum, you will not recognize it as such. Instead, you will simply perceive the red patch to be a red flower. Indeed, perceiving the red patch to be a red flower is not incorrect, but it is not as *precise* as perceiving it to be a chrysanthemum. Someone who possesses the concept "chrysanthemum," will presumably be able to recognize the red patch as a chrysanthemum. So what this person is seeing is more precise, more accurate, than what you are seeing.

Thus, the concepts or general terms that we possess can make our perception more or less precise. Think of the general terms, the concepts that you possess, as windows that allow you to perceive the manifold of features that the world has to offer. The more windows (i.e., concepts) one possesses, the more features one can perceive, and the more features one can perceive, the richer one's perception of the world.

However, the windows through which you perceive the world might be muddied and dark, and some of them might distort some of the features of the world. The concepts through which we perceive the world, in other words, might be *inaccurate*. For instance, you could possess the concept "chrysanthemum,' *but your beliefs about this concept might be false.* For instance, you might wrongly believe that this is a perennial flower, that it blooms year round. This would be incorrect since chrysanthemums are seasonal flowers. Thus, when you recognized a chrysanthemum in the garden, you would wrongly believe that you are perceiving a perennial flower, due to the fact that your beliefs about the concept are false. Although your concept of "chrysanthemum" would allow you to recognize the red patch as such, your glimpse at this slice of the world would be distorted and

73

inaccurate. Thus, in order to perceive the world as clearly as possible, one's general terms have to be *accurate*, and hence one's beliefs about that concept must be true. One's conceptual windows have to be translucent, transparent, so as to let all the light in, if one's perception of the world is going to be accurate.

Now remember that Socrates showed to others not only that some of their moral beliefs were false, but also, that they could not even adequately provide definitions of moral terms. And now that you understand that one perceives the world through beliefs and concepts, you can see how dangerous it is for one to have false moral beliefs and inaccurate moral concepts. For if one's moral beliefs are false, and if one does not possess clear and precise moral terms, then one's perception of the moral dimensions of the world is distorted and inaccurate. And Euthyphro, who cannot even state, unproblematically, what "holiness" is, and who has inconsistent beliefs about this term, actually thinks that he knows what it is, and that he accurately perceives holiness in the world. In fact, he is so convinced of this, that he is willing to prosecute his father for murder! But Socrates shows Euthyphro that his beliefs about this concept are inconsistent, and that he cannot even clearly say what holiness is. In pointing this out to Euthyphro, Socrates is helping him to see that he is most likely *misperceiving* what he is doing as holy. It is no surprise that after talking to Socrates, Euthyphro decides not to prosecute his father.

Nevertheless, even though Euthyphro's concept of holiness is muddied, Socrates believed that Euthyphro's conception of "holiness" could be improved. For insofar as the *elenchos* enables one to clean up and sharpen one's conceptions of moral terms, then it also allows one to sharpen one's *perceptions* of moral terms. Socrates believed that, although Euthyphro's perception of things could never be completely accurate, he could, nevertheless, improve his moral perception. And he could do so by using the *elenchos*.

The *elenchos* is indeed quite a powerful agent that can be used help one to perceive the moral dimensions of the world more clearly. And although we can never be certain that our moral perception is completely accurate, the *elenchos* reduces the degree to which our moral perception is inaccurate.

Ultimately, Socrates finds the *elenchos* beneficial since it makes one's moral perceptions more accurate. Indeed, by eliminating the false beliefs in one's belief set, and by sharpening one's definitions of moral concepts, one's moral perception becomes much more accurate. With this improved perception of the moral dimensions of the world, one can then lead a more moral, and hence happy life. For this reason, Socrates claimed that the unexamined life is not worth living.

Now that you can see that Socrates actually helped others to perceive correctly, it is indeed distressing that misperceptions were ultimately responsible for his trial and conviction. Socrates understood all too well that the Athenians' moral perception was dangerously inaccurate. And he accordingly devoted his life to remedying this situation. It is heart-breaking, tragic and ironic that Socrates' devotion to the improvement of others' moral perception, was misperceived as evil.

Questions for Review:

1. Which logical techniques enable one to show that a moral belief is false?
2. What is a logical consequence of a statement? Provide some examples?
3. What does it mean for one's beliefs to be inconsistent? Provide some examples of inconsistent statements.
4. What is a counterexample? Provide some examples.
5. What are the two senses of ignorance that Socrates uses the *elenchos* to reveal? Describe them.
6. How precisely, did Socrates show that his interlocutors' definitions were faulty?
7. Why is wrong with the common sense belief that perception is a passive activity?
8. In what way does being subject to the Socratic *elenchos* actually lessen the degree to which one is ignorant?
9. What is the relationship between the *elenchos* and perception?
10. Why does Socrates claim that, the unexamined life is not worth living?

Discussion Questions

1. Given Socrates' definition of "ignorance," do you think his correct when he claims that all human beings are ignorant? Why or why not?

75

2. Is there any value in repeatedly asking the question, What makes all and only actions morally right? Defend your answer.

3. Try to think of some examples from your own life that illustrate that perception is not a completely passive activity.

Endnotes

[1] All translations of *Meno* are provided by W.K.C. Guthrie

4

The End of the Examined Life

Plato's *Crito*

Socrates' ability to reveal the ignorance of his interlocutors so frustrated them, that they sentenced him to death. This is tragic, given that the *elenchos* had beneficial results. For in cross-examining and refuting the moral views of others, Socrates was only trying to improve them, to help them to perceive correctly, and hence to lead better, happier lives. Insofar as he was perceived to be a threat to Athens, Socrates was tragically misperceived.

As Socrates' friends and disciples realized that his conviction was a travesty of justice, they sought to rescue Socrates from his death sentence. In Plato's dialogue *Crito*, Socrates' friend Crito offers Socrates the opportunity to escape (*Crito* 45b-c). Of course, most people would jump at the chance of escaping a death sentence. Socrates, however, does not. Socrates says that he cannot escape unless it would be morally right for him to do so. So before escaping, Socrates first needs to determine whether doing so would be morally right. In the *Apology*, Socrates claims that a human being only has one thing to consider in performing any action, namely, whether one is acting rightly or wrongly (*Apology* 28c). This is repeated in the *Crito*, when Socrates says that his duty is to consider just one question, whether it would be right to escape, or whether it would be wrong (*Crito* 48c). So, after hearing Crito's idea, Socrates claims:

> ...we must consider whether we ought to follow your advice or not...it has always been my nature never to accept advice from any of my friends unless reflection shows that it is the best course that reason offers. I cannot abandon the arguments which I used to hold in the past simply because this accident has happened to me; they seem to me to be much as they were, and I respect and regard the same arguments now as before. So unless we can find better arguments on this occasion, you can be quite sure that I shall not agree with you...(*Crito* 46b-c)[1]

Socrates implies that the moral arguments that he has followed for his entire life, are telling him that it is *wrong* to escape. As he says, he will escape only if arguments better than his are discovered. And as you know, Socrates chooses not to escape, and hence fails to discover moral arguments that are better than his. In order to see clearly why Socrates believes that it is wrong to escape, let's get clear on what, precisely, a moral argument is.

Moral Arguments

Think of a moral argument as a reason for acting in a way that one believes to be morally right. Moral arguments are the cognitive components involved in a moral action. Hence, the type of behavior that we categorize as moral or immoral, springs from moral arguments.

There are two different components involved in a moral argument. Moral arguments include both *moral principles* and *acts of recognition or perception*. Let us take a moment to briefly discuss both of these components, so that we can better understand Socrates' claims in the *Crito*.

Moral Principles

A moral principle is simply a sentence that specifies that a particular action is right or wrong. Some examples of moral principles are:

1. It is wrong to return harm for harm
2. It is wrong to steal
3. One should obey one's superiors
4. One should live the examined life

All of us act on the basis of moral principles. Most people, however, are not even conscious of the principles that are assumed in their actions.

Suppose that you have an important chemistry exam for which you need to study. Although you have had about a month to study for this exam, you have waited until the night before the exam to do so. Now also suppose it is a Thursday night, and that some of your friends are going out that evening. They ask you to go, and you decide to go with them. In deciding to go out with your friends rather than study, you act on the basis of a moral principle. Although you are probably not immediately aware of this principle, you *could* become aware of it, if you stopped to think about it. Presumably the moral principle which leads to you to go out with your friends says something like, It is better for me to have fun than it is to study or, One should pursue what is most pleasurable, and avoid what is painful. All of our moral arguments and hence actions, involve one or more moral principles.

Recognitional Acts

As stated above, moral principles are just one of the components of moral arguments. Recognitional acts are also involved in moral arguments. A recognitional act is simply the act of perceiving some feature of the world as an instance of the concept or concepts that one possesses. To return to our chrysanthemum example from chapter three, imagine two people walking in a garden, one possesses the concepts "chrysanthemum," "flower," and "seasonal." But the other person, who, suppose, is a one year old child, does not. They walk through the garden and see in it, *a red feature of the world.* And the one who perceives this red feature *as a chrysanthemum,* and *as a seasonal flower,* recognizes this feature of the world as an instance of her concepts, "chrysanthemum," "flower," and "seasonal". The recognitional act of the child however, is much simpler. For the child simply perceives the red feature of the world that is in the garden, *as a bunch of red things.*

So the concepts that you possess will determine what you

79

perceive the various features of the world to be. We saw in the last chapter that one does not passively perceive the world, it is not as if the world is like a movie and our senses "take it all in." Rather, one perceives the world *through* one's beliefs and concepts. We perceive different slices of the world as instances of the concepts that we possess. Now let's name this type of perception, *perceiving as*. The kind of perception involved in a recognitional act, therefore, is *perceiving as*.

Perceiving As

"Perceiving as" is a ubiquitous type of perception. For when we "perceive as," we perceive the features of the world as instances of the concepts that we possess. We do this with everything. We perceive water as wet and as cold. We perceive certain individuals as funny, as sarcastic and as patriotic. We perceive grass as green and fire as hot. And, as you know, we perceive certain actions as moral, and certain actions as immoral.

"Perceiving as" plays an important role in moral arguments, and hence in *moral behavior*. Consider the following example, if I stop myself from stealing my neighbor's money, it is not enough that I utter the principle "It is wrong to steal." I also have to recognize that breaking into my neighbor's house and removing the money from within it *counts* as an act of stealing. In other words, I have to perceive the act of breaking, entering, and walking away with my neighbor's money *as* an act of stealing. So in the above example, when I stop myself from stealing, there are two cognitive components involved. On the one hand, I believe the moral principle "It is wrong to steal," and on the other hand, I perceive my removing money from my neighbor's house *as* an act of stealing. Since, according to one of my moral principles, stealing is wrong, and since I perceive my removing money from my neighbor's house *as* an act of stealing, then I prevent myself from removing my neighbor's money from her house.

A moral argument, then, is a reason for acting that contains at least one moral principle, and at least one act of "perceiving as". A moral argument says something like, It is always wrong to steal, this is an act of stealing (I perceive this as an act of stealing), so it is wrong to do this.

Moral Disagreement

Both moral principles and "perceiving as" are components of moral arguments, and people disagree about both. However, there seems to be more disagreement pertaining to acts of recognition or "perceiving as," than there is disagreement pertaining to general moral principles.

Consider the contemporary debate about the legality of abortion: both sides in the abortion debate believe the general principle that murder is wrong, but whereas some of them recognize or perceive abortion as an act of murder, others do not. We could also say that all Athenians agreed on the moral principle that says, "someone who corrupts the youth should be condemned to death." But whereas some perceived Socrates *as* a corrupter of youth, others did not. So people can agree on their moral principles, but disagree in their perceptions. In fact, most moral disagreements are about perceptions rather than principles. Socrates recognizes this in the *Euthyphro,* when he claims that, it is not the moral principle, "the wrongdoer should pay the penalty" about which people disagree. Rather, it is the perception that a particular person or act is wrong. And Euthyphro agrees with this (*Euthyphro* 8d).

When there is disagreement about how and what to perceive a feature of the world as, people are disagreeing about which concept or concepts that feature of the world is an instance of. For some, that feature of the world in which there is a person getting an abortion is an instance of the concept "evil," and for others it is not. And you know from your own experience, that people vehemently disagree in their "perceiving as" of the moral features of the world: we do not all perceive the same actions as moral, and the same actions as immoral. Indeed, disagreements about the moral concepts that a person or an action instantiates, are perhaps the most serious disagreements that human beings have with one another. These disagreements have led to war, to the enslavement of whole peoples, and to the killing of innocents.

In Socrates' time as in ours, people disagreed in their perceptions of the instances of moral concepts. Although some might conclude from this that morality is a completely subjective affair, and relative to the perceiver (i.e., "an action is right if it seems right to me"), Socrates did not accept this view. For Socrates believed that some people *incorrectly* perceive the moral dimensions of the world, and hence that one could "perceive as" incorrectly. Remember that Socrates claimed

81

that those who perceived him as immoral perceived him incorrectly. This shows that Socrates believed that, although people disagree in their perception of the moral dimension of the world, this does not mean that there is not a right way to perceive this dimension. In fact, Socrates believed that the majority of people incorrectly perceived the moral dimension of the world. In his view, the majority of people were walking around as if they were drunk, in a fog, mistaking immoral actions for moral actions, and moral people for ones that were immoral. Why do you think he believed this given what you have recently learned about the interaction of concepts such as "justice," and the perceptions of just acts?

The Disagreement between Socrates and Crito

Now that we understand that both moral principles and "perceptions as" are components of moral arguments, and that people can disagree about both, let's return to the *Crito* to see about what, precisely, Socrates and Crito are disagreeing. When Socrates tells Crito in the above passage that, he cannot abandon the arguments by which he has lived, he is referring to both the *general principles* and his *"perceptions as"* that figure in these arguments. He is saying that he cannot abandon either the principles, or the way that he perceives things, unless Crito shows him a better way. And as you know, Socrates chose not to escape. Crito, then, failed to show Socrates that there is a better way.

At the beginning of the *Crito*, Socrates and Crito disagree about whether Socrates' act of escaping is morally right. Thus, they are disagreeing about whether Socrates' act of escaping is an instance of the concept, "morally right." Crito tries to convince Socrates that it is, and hence that he should escape. In order to do so, Crito argues that Socrates would behave wrongly in choosing to remain in prison. He says:

> ...Socrates, I don't even feel that it is right for you to do what you are doing, throwing away your life when you might save it. You are doing your best to treat yourself in exactly the same way as your enemies would, or rather did, when they wanted to ruin you. What is more, it seems to me that you are letting your sons down too. You have it in your power to finish their bringing up and education, and instead you are proposing to desert them...It strikes me that you are taking the

line of least resistance, whereas you ought to make the choice of good man and a brave one, considering that you profess to have made goodness your object all through life. (*Crito* 45c-d)

Look at the end of the argument. Crito states that Socrates should escape since doing so would be the morally right thing to do. For he says to Socrates, You ought to make the choice of a good man and a brave one. Crito, therefore, is assuming the principle "One should act rightly and bravely." And of course, Socrates agrees with the moral principle that one should act rightly and bravely. But Socrates disagrees with Crito's view that he would *not* be acting rightly and bravely if he escaped from prison. For it seems to him that it would be wrong to escape. The fact that Socrates and Crito agree on the principle "one should act rightly or bravely," but disagree about whether Socrates would be acting rightly and bravely if he remained in prison, shows that they are not disagreeing about the principles that they hold, but rather about their *perceptions as*.

Some Moral Arguments are Better than Others

Given that Socrates and Crito disagree on whether Socrates' escaping is morally right, why does Socrates need to be convinced by Crito that Crito's way is better? In other words, why doesn't Socrates just automatically assume that Crito is correct and that he, Socrates, is wrong? Why is Socrates at all confident that his perception is accurate, given his disavowal of wisdom?

Remember that Socrates has led the examined life. That is, Socrates has examined his own moral views, in the same way that he examined those of his interlocutors'. Socrates has spent his life determining the consequences of his moral beliefs, and eliminating any beliefs that gave rise to inconsistencies in his belief set. And Socrates has also spent his life sharpening his conceptions (and therefore perceptions) of moral terms. The principles by which Socrates has lived are the result of a myriad of elenctic examinations. And the recognitional acts that figure in Socrates' moral arguments spring from concepts that have been sharpened by the *elenchos*. Socrates has very good reasons for believing that his perception is accurate, or at least more accurate, than Crito's. The conceptual windows through which Socrates peers out into the world are clean and clear, whereas Crito's as you will see, are not.

Nevertheless, Socrates is willing to admit that his arguments –

his principles and his recognitional acts – may be wrong. For he suggests that he and Crito *might* be able to discover better arguments. Socrates is not claiming that he knows, with certainty, that his arguments are the best ones. The *elenchos* cannot give Socrates definitive knowledge. For it cannot show that a moral principle is correct, and one can always sharpen one's definitions further. Remember, the *elenchos* can only indicate that a moral principle or a definition is *not* correct,[2] and so just as Socrates' divine voice only told him what *not* to do, the *elenchos* tells Socrates and his interlocutors only what *not* to believe. This accords with Socrates' disavowal of wisdom. He does not know definitively that his arguments are the best ones, for not even the *elenchos* can tell him that. And Socrates could never have definitive knowledge, since real wisdom is the property of God (*Apology* 23a). Socrates, then, leaves open the possibility that there might be other arguments that are better than his, but that have yet to be discovered. Socrates is even willing to entertain the possibility that *Crito's* arguments may be better than his.

Nevertheless, in the *Crito*, Socrates uses the *elenchos* to show that Crito's perception that it would be right for Socrates to escape, is incorrect. And Crito can find no reason to disagree with Socrates. Let us see how Socrates convinces Crito that in perceiving Socrates' escape as morally right, Crito is perceiving incorrectly.

Getting Crito to see what He Believes

In order to convince Crito that it would be wrong for Socrates to escape, Socrates reminds Crito that both of them have lived according to the following principles:

1. It is always wrong to harm another (*Crito* 49b)

2. It is always wrong to break one's agreements, if they are just (*Crito* 49e)

Socrates explains to Crito, that if he escapes, he would be violating both of these principles. For he would violate the second principle, because he has agreed to accept all of the city's decisions. Socrates claims that he has accepted this agreement when he decided to live in Athens, and to raise his children in this city. So, since escaping would be violating the city's legal decision that Socrates should be put to death, it would be wrong for Socrates to escape. Even worse, if Socrates violated his agreement with the city, he would also be harming the city. But harming the city is prohibited according to Socrates' principle that one should never harm another. So, Socrates concludes that it would be morally wrong for him to escape. His reasoning is as follows:

1. It is always wrong to harm another
1a. If Socrates escaped, he would harm the city (*Crito* 51a)
    It is wrong for Socrates to escape

2. It is always wrong to break one's agreements, if they are just
2a. Socrates' agreement to accept all of Athens' decisions is just (*Crito* 50d-52d)
2b. Athens has decided to condemn Socrates to death
2c. If Socrates escaped, he would be breaking his agreement
     with the city (*Crito* 52d)
     It is wrong for Socrates to escape

After listening to Socrates' arguments, Crito realizes that he misperceived the situation at the beginning of the dialogue. For at the beginning of the dialogue, Crito perceives Socrates' decision to remain in prison as wrong. But now, after understanding Socrates' arguments, he realizes that it is right for Socrates to remain in prison. This is yet another illustration that shows that perception is not a completely passive activity. Understanding Socrates' argument *changes* Crito's perception of Socrates decision to remain in prison, and he is forced to agree with Socrates.

Crito originally perceives Socrates' refusal to escape as morally wrong, because he Crito *has forgotten* some of the other principles by which he lives. Socrates, in effect, reminds Crito of some his principles; namely, that it is always wrong to harm another, and that it is wrong to break one's agreements. Once Crito is reminded of these principles, he realizes that it is wrong for Socrates to escape. For Socrates gets Crito *to see what he believes.* Thus, at the end of the dialogue, Socrates tells Crito to give up trying to convince Socrates that he should escape, since God is pointing out that it would be wrong for Socrates to do so (*Crito* 54e). Socrates is presumably talking about Apollo, the God of health, who commanded Socrates to live the examined life.

Perhaps you find Socrates' arguments implausible. And perhaps you remain unconvinced that it was wrong for Socrates to escape. If you are unpersuaded by Socrates' argument, he would be willing to listen to you. However, you would have to show him that his arguments are flawed for some reason. In other words, you would have to show Socrates that his principles contradict some of his other beliefs, that his definitions are subject to counterexamples, and so on. And given that Socrates has lived his entire examining himself and his moral views, it would be unlikely if you could do this. But even if you could, your task of refuting Socrates would still not be complete. For you would also have to provide him with alternative arguments that had no flaws. You would have to provide him with arguments which had sound moral principles and accurate recognitional acts, and which claimed that Socrates should escape. Crito could do none of these things – he was unable to come up with any arguments better than Socrates'. Nor was Socrates able to think of arguments that were better than the ones that he had been following for his entire life. For this reason, both Crito and Socrates concluded that it was morally wrong for Socrates to escape.

Morality and Reason

The fact that both Socrates and Crito conclude that Socrates should face death because this is act is supported by the best moral argument, demonstrates that both of them believed that there was a profound connection between reason and morality. Accordingly, at one point in the *Crito*, Socrates states that he only accepts advice from his friends unless this advice is "the best course that reason offers." This claim demonstrates precisely why Socrates examines arguments in order to determine whether actions are right or wrong. For Socrates believes that an *action* is *morally right* if it has the *best reasons* or *arguments* on its side. This claim is an extremely important one, for it was not only the driving force behind all of Socrates' actions, but it has also been one of the most influential moral insights in the entire history of Western thought. In the 1800's, this idea received expression in the moral philosophy of the great German philosopher, Immanuel Kant, and continues to be agreed upon by the majority of philosophers even today. Although there are some important differences between Kant and Socrates, like Socrates, Kant believed that morally right actions were ones which followed good reasons.[3]

Let us take a moment to point out just how different Socrates' view of morality, of ethical behavior, is different from ours. For one thing, most of us never bother to ask what words like "rightness," "justice," and "virtue" mean. But Socrates believed that this was one of the most important questions that one could ask. For asking these sorts of questions allowed one to sharpen their definitions of these concepts, which in turn, would improve one's perception of the various instances of these concepts. The emphasis placed on the improvement of one's moral perception is virtually absent from the way that most of us approach morality. For most of us our unaware that our perception of reality is mediated by concepts, which may or may not be accurate.

A further difference between Socrates' and our approach to morality is the emphasis that he places on reason and rational reflection. Think about some of the moral principles by which you live. Perhaps you think that it is always wrong to kill an innocent person. And perhaps you believe that it is wrong to use another person as a mere means to get something else. But where do your principles come from? How did you acquire your moral principles, your standards of rightness and wrongness? For most people, moral principles are taught by one's culture or religion. Thus, for most, moral principles come from the outside, and one is simply conditioned to believe them. Because of this, many people believe that to be moral is simply to follow the moral principles that have been taught to them by others.

But for Socrates morality was something completely different. Socrates surely recognizes that moral principles *can* come from one's society, or from one's religion, but he does not believe that they *should* come from either of these places. Rather, one's moral principles should come from *reason*, from reflection and examination. Moral principles should be tested, and moral concepts should be sharpened with repeated definition attempts. And now you should understand why Socrates thinks this. For if one's moral principles and concepts remain unexamined, then it is virtually certain that one's perception of the moral dimensions of the world is inaccurate. Thus, Socrates believes that morality is a matter of consulting reason because reason enables one to streamline one's beliefs and concepts so that one can perceive more accurately. Just think about this claim for

87

a minute and you will start to realize just how different it is from the way that we conceive of morality.

The fact that Socrates believes that the rightness of an action is determined by the reasons for performing it, shows more clearly why he believed that it was wrong for him to escape. For when an act springs from good reasons, then it is more probable (though not guaranteed), that one is perceiving correctly. And Socrates is perceiving his act of escaping through beliefs that have been tested and concepts that have been sharpened by reason. Consequently, it is quite clear to him that it would be wrong for him to escape. Socrates, who has been able to know himself better by living the examined life, sees that his true self is something rational, indeed, *is reason*. And it is *reason* that tells Socrates that it is wrong to escape. And although Socrates cannot know himself, know reason, completely, what he does know of it is telling him that he should not escape.

Socrates' Eudaimonism

There is a further feature of Socrates' view of morality that is so very different than ours, and that needs to be mentioned. For once we understand this feature, we will see why Socrates was not only confident that it would be wrong for him to escape, but also why, in the face of death, Socrates remained calm, rational, and even at peace with himself.

In the *Crito*, Socrates and Crito both agree that the most important thing is not simply to live, but to live well (*Crito* 48b). Immediately after saying this, they agree on the further claim that to live well means the same thing to live rightly (*Crito* 48b). These claims indicate that Socrates was a *eudaimonist* (pronounced "you-dime-own-ist"). The word "*eudaimonia*" (you-dime-own-ia) is often translated as "happiness," but this is a misleading translation. For we think of happiness as something that comes and goes, but *eudaimonia* is not like this. *Eudaimonia* is the point that one reaches when one attains the completion and perfection of their nature. Once one reaches this point, it cannot not be lost, and one cannot not go back.

For many Greek philosophers, all human beings are ultimately trying to achieve *eudaimonia*. Thus, *Eudaimonia* was believed to be the goal for which all human beings strive, that thing for which we are all searching. The Greeks believed that the desire for *eudaimonia* is in everybody, and hence that everybody yearns and searches for it, and hence for the perfection of themselves. Accordingly, the perfection of oneself was believed to be the most pleasurable and complete state that a human being a reach, and unlike other states, being *eudaimon* was permanent. Aristotle's great ethical work the *Nicomachean Ethics* concerns *eudaimonia*. Aristotle wants to know what it is, and how it can be achieved, and he provides answers to these questions in the *Nicomachean Ethics*.

Socrates believed that one was *eudaimon* if they had perfected themselves. Remember, though, that Socrates realized that most people did not even know themselves: most of their words and deeds come from some alien place, which is not even their own. This is what Socrates was ultimately trying to show with the *elenchos*, as you now know. For Socrates showed to others that if they thought about their beliefs and actions, they would realize that they were wrong, and would say and do things entirely differently. It is only the space of reason and reflection, from which one's words and deeds are really their own.

Socrates desired *eudaimonia* just as others did. But unlike others, Socrates realized by living the examined life, that he and others' were truly *rational*, and that the desire for *eudaimonia* came from a rational creature, that was yearning to be perfected. But most people do not realize that they are rational creatures with rational desires, and hence the reason within them hides behind a veil of muddied concepts, false beliefs, and ignoble appetites. People believe that it is money, fame, or political power that they truly desire. Sadly, most people do not realize who they really are, and what they truly desire. However, Socrates and others after him believed that the human soul is something rational, and that this rational soul yearns to be perfected so that it can peer out into the world and see it as richly and as accurately as possible.

Socrates did not claim that he had perfected his rational soul, and he seems to have believed that it was impossible to do so. Nevertheless, Socrates believed that trying to do so was the best thing that any human being could do, and this is why he lived as he did, examining and refuting others, helping them to see who they really are, and what they really desire and believe. Socrates does this even in the face of death when he shows to Crito that they really believe that it is right for Socrates to remain and accept the death penalty.

In believing that to live well is the same thing to live rightly, Socrates provides a powerful incentive for being moral, and hence for being rational. For all those people who ask Why should I be moral? Why should I be rational? and Why should I lived the examined life? Socrates answers, because this is what you truly desire, this is what you are truly yearning for, and doing so helps you to perfect yourself.

Socrates, who lived more than two thousand years ago had important insights into moral behavior that have been forgotten in the twentieth century. Realizing the significant role that perception plays in our moral actions, and realizing that the moral perception of most people was incorrect, Socrates lived and died trying to show people that philosophy, that elenctic examination, could provide a human being with a trained eye for recognizing the moral dimensions of the world. Socrates taught us that reason should be used not primarily to contemplate the universe, and the workings of nature, but to contemplate our moral conceptions so that we could live better, happier lives, and know our true selves. For these reasons, Socrates claimed that the unexamined life is not worth living.

Questions for Review:

1. What is a moral argument?
2. What are the two components of a moral argument?
3. What are some examples that show that people disagree about moral principles?
4. What are some examples that show that people disagree about their perception of particular moral acts?
5. About what, do Socrates and Crito disagree?
6. How does Socrates show that Crito's view about Socrates' escape is incorrect?
7. What would you need to do in order to convince Socrates that his view that escaping would be wrong, is incorrect.
8. According to Socrates, what is the relationship between morality and reason?
9. What is *eudaimonia?*
10. According to Socrates, what is the connection between reason, morality, and *eudaimonia?*

Discussion Questions

1. Do you agree with Socrates' view that morality is first and foremost a matter of consulting reason, of looking at arguments? Why or why not?

2. Try to think of some examples in which people are disagreeing not about moral principles, but about the perceptions of individual actions. What, in your view, is responsible for the fact that people disagree in their perception of moral properties, in their "perceptions as"?

3. Given that people disagree in their perception of moral properties, is there any way to resolve such a disagreement? How?

If you think that someone is misperceiving a moral situation, could you convince them of that? If so, how? If not, why not?

---

[1] All translations of *Crito* are by Hugh Tredennick

[2] Sometimes, the *elenchos* cannot tell someone what not to believe. If the *elenchos* reveals that one has inconsistent beliefs, one has to determine which one to reject. Determining which principle has the fewest number of negative consequences is one way to proceed, and the *elenchos* can be used to do this.

[3] According to Kant, an action is morally right if it proceeds from a reason that one could will to be a universal law. A significant different between Socrates and Kant was that Socrates was a *eudaimonist*, whereas Kant was not. In other words, Socrates believed that we should be moral because moral activity was the absolute best activity, the most pleasant and rewarding, in which one could engage. It is not immediately clear that Kant shared this sentiment.

Bibliography

1. Arrowsmith, William (trans.) <u>Clouds</u>, in *Four Plays by Aristophanes*, Meridian, 1994
2. Benson, Hugh H., *Essays on the Philosophy of Socrates*, Oxford University Press, 1992
3. Brickhouse, Thomas and Smith, Nicholas D., *Plato's Socrates*, Oxford University Press, 1994
4. Brickhouse, Thomas and Smith, Nicholas D., *Socrates on Trial*, Princeton, 1990.
5. Guthrie, W.K.C, *Socrates*, Cambridge, 1971.
6. Hamilton, Edith and Cairns, Huntington (ed.'s) *The Collected Dialogues of Plato*, Princeton, 1961.
8. Marchant, E.C., (trans.) *Memorabilia* in *Xenophon: Memorabilia, Oeconomicus, Symposium, Apologia*, Harvard, 1923.
9. McPherran, Mark, *The Religion of Socrates*, Penn. State University Press, 1996
8. Navia, Luis E., *Socrates: The Man and His Philosophy*, Lanham, 1985.
9. Strauss, Leo, *Xenophon's Socrates*, Cornell, 1972.
10. Vlastos, Gregory (ed.), *The Philosophy of Socrates*, Garden City, 1971.